THE OPEN UNIVERSITY
Arts: A Third Level Course
The Nineteenth-century Novel and its Legacy
Unit 26

Points of View

Prepared for the Course Team by Arnold Kettle,
Joan Bellamy, Angus Calder, John Goode, Dennis Walder
and Raymond Williams

The Open University Press

Cover: Lithograph by Daumier, no. 13 of Les Bas-bleus *(The Blue-stockings), a series of satires on feminism, from* Le Charivari, *8th March 1844. '"Pardon me, sir, if I disturb you somewhat . . . but you will understand that, since I am writing a new novel at the moment, I must consult a host of ancient authors!" [The Gentleman, aside]: "Ancient authors! . . . Indeed! She really should have consulted them when they were alive—she must have been their contemporary!"' (Feminists had called for a reading room for women at the Bibliothèque Nationale in Paris.) (Reproduced by courtesy of the British Library Board)*

The Open University Press
Walton Hall, Milton Keynes
MK7 6AA

This book first published 1973 as A302 Unit 23 *The Late Nineteenth-century Novel*. This new revised edition first published 1982.

Copyright © 1973, 1982 The Open University

Designed by the Graphic Design Group of the Open University.

Printed in Great Britain by
Eyre & Spottiswoode Limited at Grosvenor Press, Portsmouth

ISBN 0 335 11066 5

This text forms part of an Open University course. The complete list of units in the course appears at the end of this text.

For general availability of supporting material referred to in this text, please write to Open University Educational Enterprises Limited, 12 Cofferidge Close, Stony Stratford, Milton Keynes MK11 1BY, Great Britain.

Further information on Open University courses may be obtained from the Admissions Office, The Open University, P.O. Box 48, Walton Hall, Milton Keynes MK7 6AB.

1.1

Contents

Introduction

(By Dennis Walder)

At various stages earlier in the course we have tried to move beyond the study of individual texts, to consider some of the thematic or formal inter-relationships between the different novels, and also the connections between these themes and general social or 'cultural' developments. This is in line with our overall aim (as announced in Unit 1), which is to consider the nineteenth-century novel not just as a series of individual texts—although that is where we always start—but also as a cultural phenomenon specific to its time and place.

In this unit, as in Units 1 and 11, our aim is to develop further some aspects of the more 'general' topics which have already been raised: partly as a way of taking stock of some of the issues touched on in more recent units; partly as a way of looking ahead to the 'Legacies' block (Units 27–32), where we will be examining a number of twentieth-century fictions with a view to finding out how much the nineteenth-century novel form changed—and how much it stayed the same—in the hands of a representative sample of the successors of Dickens, George Eliot, Tolstoy and Hardy.

What we have decided to offer here is a series of different but related perspectives or 'points of view' on some of the novels in the course, ranging from Arnold Kettle's comparison of the 'narrative method' in several different but specific passages, to John Goode's more general account of the relationship between 'narrative methods' as such and the times in which they prevail. The material offered here is intentionally varied, and written in different ways. This is because we now want to stimulate and provoke you, as an experienced reader familiar with the texts under discussion, rather than continue to guide you in the 'elementaries'. This isn't meant to sound patronizing: 'Oh good, I'm grown up, so I can be left to make up my own mind,' you might want to respond. It's more a matter of our wanting to try out different approaches and levels now that you have had a chance to get to grips with several major novels. We want you to discover which approach you find most fruitful and appropriate for yourself. All the sections are rewarding, we believe, in different ways; all have to do with, centrally, the *way* that our chosen novelists write, and to a lesser but still important extent, *why* they write in the way they do. In an Appendix we have added 'A note on realism and naturalism', contributed by Raymond Williams. It is a general piece which relates to the overall discussion, throughout the course, of the notion of 'realism'; though less concerned with the particular topics of this unit, it will give you a valuable perspective on this central notion as you now look back over the main part of the course.

The different but related meanings of the term 'point of view' suggested our title. You could call the unit a collection of 'points of view on points of view'—i.e. approaches from different formal and moral standpoints to the 'points of view' of some nineteenth-century novelists. None of the approaches is the 'last word' on its topic, by any means. And we will be continuing the discussion in Units 27–32, as you will see.

1   The novelist's narrative

(By Arnold Kettle)

Narrative and 'point of view'

> Percy Lubbock taught us forty years ago to believe that 'the art of fiction does not begin until the novelist thinks of his story as a matter to be *shown*, to be so exhibited that it will tell itself' [*The Craft of Fiction*, page 62]. He may have been in some sense right—but to say so raises more questions than it answers.
>
> Why is it that an episode 'told' by Fielding can strike us as more fully realized than many of the scenes scrupulously 'shown' by imitators of James or Hemingway? Why does some authorial commentary ruin the work in which it occurs, while the prolonged commentary of *Tristram Shandy* can still enthral us? What, after all, does an author do when he 'intrudes' to 'tell' us something about his story? Such questions force us to consider closely what happens when an author engages a reader fully with a work of fiction; they lead us to a view of fictional technique which necessarily goes far beyond the reductions that we have sometimes accepted under the concept of 'point of view'. (Wayne C. Booth, 'Telling and showing', from *The Rhetoric of Fiction*, 1961, quoted in *The Nineteenth-century Novel: Critical Essays and Documents* (Course Reader), page 54)

This section consists of the examination of four examples of fictional narrative. The first example is only marginally 'fictional' in content: but as far as *method* goes, the writer's problems are much the same as those of the novelist.

My object is to use the four passages as the basis for a discussion of some of the problems of narrative method. I use the term 'narrative method' in a very broad sense, to indicate the way the writer tells his story and to include such sub-terms as 'dramatic', 'descriptive', 'panoramic', etc. (NB   The distinction, discussed later on, between 'narrate' and 'describe' would come *within* the general heading of 'narrative method' as I use the term.) Needless to say, the discussion isn't all-inclusive but concentrates on certain aspects which lend themselves to comparison. I want to make clear what I'm *not* doing or . claiming:

(i)   I'm *not* suggesting that the passages are entirely representative of their authors. Therefore it mustn't be inferred that one can say—on the basis of this discussion—'Jane Austen always does such-and-such' or 'George Eliot's method is such-and-such'. If I generalize (as I sometimes do) about the author's method, such generalizations have to be seen within the context of this particular exercise. They *may* have more general application (I think they generally do) but you mustn't assume that.

(ii)   I'm *not* suggesting that my treatment of the passages is the only possible one, even within the terms of this particular exercise. I'm trying to link four passages written entirely independently, and this is bound to involve a certain amount of special emphasis and even, from some points of view, distortion.

The first aim in every case is to describe what the story-teller is up to, the second to consider some of the implications of the different sorts of narrative method used. I tend to move (you'll notice) from the term 'narrative method' (which involves some sort of analysis of how the writer gets his effects) to 'point of view' (which involves an assessment of the writer's stance as it more or less unconsciously determines his narrative method). I think the two are always closely linked and sometimes so near to being inseparable that one can properly shift from one to the other.

1 Saga

This passage is not from a novel but from a very early example of prose narrative, the *Icelandic Book of the Settlement*, compiled about the twelfth century, though based on material of the ninth and tenth. It is translated by Bertha S. Phillpotts and discussed in her book *Edda and Saga* (pp. 168ff.). The *Book of the Settlement* is one of the earliest known examples of prose narrative, and though it is a history or 'chronicle' (i.e. the events have the status of being true) the writer faces problems of narration of a kind comparable to those of the novelist.

Here is the passage:

> Hallbjorn . . . married Hallgerd, daughter of Odd of Tunga: they were with Odd the first winter. Snaebjorn 'Boar' was there. There were no loving relations between Hallbjorn and his wife. In the spring Hallbjorn made ready to move, but while he was moving Odd, Hallgerd's father, went from the house to the hot springs at Reykjaholt, where his sheep-sheds were: he did not wish to be present when Hallbjorn left, because he had his doubts whether Hallgerd would be willing to go with him. Odd had always smoothed over differences between the two.
>
> When Hallbjorn had saddled their horses he went to the bower. Hallgerd was sitting on the cross-bench combing her hair: it fell all about her and on the floor. She and Hallgerd Longbreeks [who married Gunnar of Njal's Saga] had the loveliest hair of any women in Iceland. Hallbjorn bade her rise up and come. She sat where she was and did not speak: then he took hold of her and she would not be lifted. Three times he did it.
>
> Then, standing before her, he uttered a verse:
>
>> 'Elm[1] with arms unyielding,
>> I win from eyes averted,
>> from look by locks hidden
>> no glance of love for answer!
>> White and wan with pining
>> unending woe attends me,
>> thou linen-clad lady!
>> Alas! O heart's sore sorrow!'
>
> Then he wound her hair in his hand and tried to pull her from the bench, but she sat and did not yield. Then he drew his sword and struck off her head. He went out and rode away. There were three of them and they had laden packhorses with them. There were not many people in the house, and a message was sent forthwith to Odd. Snaebjorn was at Kjalvarastad, and Odd sent a man to him, bidding him see about the pursuit: he himself, he said, would have no part in it.
>
> [1]Trees were often used as metaphors for human beings in skaldic verse.

When you have read the passage carefully, make notes on the following topics:

(i)   How are the feelings of the characters conveyed to the reader?

(ii)   What features of the narrative method (not the subject-matter) strike you?

(iii)   Do you see any likely relationships between the writer's method of narration and the material he is recording?

(NB You don't have to know anything about mediaeval Iceland to answer these questions. It may, however, be useful to know that breaking into verse at certain points of the story is a common feature of early Icelandic sagas.)

Discussion

(i) The feelings of the characters are conveyed almost solely by their actions. We are told the minimum about the marital situation and, apart from the lines uttered in verse, are given no description of how the people feel. And even in the lines of verse there is no *analysis* of feelings.

(ii) Bertha Phillpotts puts it like this:

> As we read it we feel as if we were looking on at the enacted tragedy. The technique is wholly dramatic. The hopes and fears and motives of the actors are explained by their actions alone, except that we are briefly told why the father went away. His inaction after the tragedy shows that he knows that his daughter has been faithless: he cannot feel justified in taking vengeance for her—and yet wants it taken. So he sends to the lover. The girl's own feelings are made clear to us without a word of explanation from herself or the story-teller; and so are her husband's. His verse heightens the emotional effect but is not necessary to explain the conflict in his mind. The mention of the other Hallgerd is not an idle digression: it hints at tragedy to come, for that other Hallgerd caused the death of her husband . . .
>
> The Saga-teller utterly rejects the convention of the modern novel, that the author is a kind of god who knows, not only everything that is spoken in private, but also all that is going on in the minds of his characters— even of what those personages are not conscious . . .
>
> The story unfolds as to an onlooker, watching the doings of his neighbours and coming, as in real life, gradually to understand their motives. (ibid., pp. 170–72)

This method of narration, it should be noted, depends above all on two conventions: that events are related chronologically, in their right order, and that the narrator chooses the relevant actions.

(iii) Bertha Phillpott's reference to the 'other Hallgerd' (which those of us who don't know about Icelandic sagas couldn't possibly have got) gives us one suggestive hint. This particular sort of narrative can work fully only if the reader (or, more likely, listener) is familiar in some sense with the situations being described. The references in the narrative, in other words, must be to some part of the listener's experience or culture. The story-teller must be able to assume a common basis of knowledge and tradition which his hearers share.

This works not only for specific references like the one to Hallgerd Long-breeks, but also for general social ethics and values. It is *assumed* by this narrator (and by his audience) that a husband whose wife is unfaithful and disobeys him will consider himself justified in killing her, and that her lover will seek revenge: also, more subtly, that her father *wouldn't* feel justified in avenging his daughter in such circumstances since she has broken an important rule of social behaviour. One can say, then, that this narrative method presupposes a fairly simple social order with an agreed moral code and also a society in which everyone will be likely to know everyone else and to share much common experience: a very *public* society, in fact, where the distinction between public and private life is not a hard and fast one.

The Icelandic Saga . . . tells us all that anybody need know about the working of the characters' minds, without ever appearing to know more than can be known by any intelligent person in the countryside. *The watching countryside is the real secret of their success; that and the choice of significant incidents and a rigid adherence to the order of events.* (ibid., pp. 171–72; my italics)

2 Jane Austen

The passage is from *Mansfield Park* (Penguin ed., Chapter 21, pp. 211–12). You will know the context. Sir Thomas Bertram has just returned to Mansfield Park, and the goings-on around the performance of *Lovers' Vows* have been brought to an abrupt end.

Sir Thomas's return made a striking change in the ways of the family, independent of Lovers' Vows. Under his government, Mansfield was an altered place. Some members of their society sent away and the spirits of many others saddened, it was all sameness and gloom, compared with the past; a sombre family-party rarely enlivened. There was little intercourse with the Parsonage. Sir Thomas drawing back from intimacies in general, was particularly disinclined, at this time, for any engagements but in one quarter. The Rushworths were the only addition to his own domestic circle which he could solicit.

Edmund did not wonder that such should be his father's feelings, nor could he regret any thing but the exclusion of the Grants. 'But they,' he observed to Fanny, 'have a claim. They seem to belong to us—they seem to be part of ourselves. I could wish my father were more sensible of their very great attention to my mother and sisters while he was away. I am afraid they may feel themselves neglected. But the truth is that my father hardly knows them. They had not been here a twelvemonth when he left England. If he knew them better, he would value their society as it deserves, for they are in fact exactly the sort of people he would like. We are sometimes a little in want of animation among ourselves; my sisters seem out of spirits, and Tom is certainly not at his ease. Dr and Mrs Grant would enliven us, and make our evenings pass away with more enjoyment even to my father.'

'Do you think so?' said Fanny. 'In my opinion, my uncle would not like *any* addition. I think he values the very quietness you speak of, and that the repose of his own family-circle is all he wants. And it does not appear to me that we are more serious than we used to be; I mean before my uncle went abroad. As well as I can recollect, it was always much the same. There was never much laughing in his presence; or, if there is any difference, it is not more I think than such an absence has a tendency to produce at first. There must be a sort of shyness. But I cannot recollect that our evenings formerly were ever merry, except when my uncle was in town. No young people's are, I suppose, when those they look up to are at home.'

'I believe you are right, Fanny,' was his reply, after a short consideration. 'I believe our evenings are rather returned to what they were, than assuming a new character. The novelty was in their being lively.—Yet, how strong the impression that only a few weeks will give! I have been feeling as if we had never lived so before.'

'I suppose I am graver than other people,' said Fanny. 'The evenings do not appear long to me. I love to hear my uncle talk of the West Indies. I could listen to him for an hour together. It entertains *me* more than many other things have done—but then I am unlike other people I dare say.'

'Why should you dare say *that*? (smiling)—Do you want to be told that you are only unlike other people in being more wise and discreet? But when did you or any body ever get a compliment from me, Fanny? Go to my father if you want to be complimented. He will satisfy you. Ask your uncle what he thinks, and you will hear compliments enough; and though they may be chiefly on your person, you must put up with it, and trust to his seeing as much beauty of mind in time.'

Such language was so new to Fanny that it quite embarrassed her.

When you have read the passage carefully, make notes on the following topics:

(i)   How would you compare the narrative style with that of passage 1 (the Icelandic saga)?

(ii)   Would you describe Jane Austen's narrative stance as 'god-like'?[1]

(iii)   How far do the style and tone depend on (a) shared, (b) individual moral discriminations, and how do these problems emerge in Jane Austen's use of language? (To put this last question in another way: how far is Jane Austen's style of narrative determined by the general social situation within which her individual sensibility operates?)

Discussion

(i)   Perhaps one might start with the word *intimate*. Jane Austen takes us right into a situation, whereas the Icelander had let us see it from the outside. *His* narrative presents people as they appear to others and, since the society he is describing is, as has been suggested, a very public one, the reader is prepared to agree that in knowing the way these people behave one knows all one needs to know about them. Jane Austen, on the other hand, is concerned, among other things, with exploring differences between appearance and reality. Is Mansfield really dull, as Edmund evidently feels, or are the evenings spent in Sir Thomas's company as delightful as Fanny would maintain? Such questions, obviously, belong to a closer, more intimate and more sophisticated world than that of Hallbjorn and Hallgerd. There justice is a rough and ready matter: in the Bertrams' corner of England in 1816 it involves subtler, though not necessarily more fundamental, discriminations. Sir Thomas's moral code may not be in every sense much more flexible than Hallbjorn's, but he is certainly operating within a sphere that gives him and his family considerably more room for manoeuvre. The dramatic element in Jane Austen's narrative is therefore less obvious, less public: it has been transferred, one might say, into the minds and feelings of the characters. We do not *know* what poor Hallgerd thought just before her head was chopped off, but we can guess: we do know, as Bertha Phillpotts says, all we need know. But we couldn't possibly understand the full complexity of Fanny's and Edmund's reactions to Sir Thomas's régime at Mansfield Park simply by watching their actions. In the Icelandic situation words are unnecessary (Hallbjorn has literally nothing to *discuss* with Hallgerd at this point!). Talk at Mansfield, on the other hand, is all-important, and the peculiarity of the talk in a Jane Austen novel is that it is very finely and precisely threaded with action and experience. The characters act and also discuss their own and each other's actions and the reader is all the time able to test the adequacy of their talk—and often its sincerity—by referring it to the situations and behaviour that are being talked about. Thus Fanny's rather complacent report in favour of those boring evenings at Mansfield is *tested* by Edmund's suggestion that

---

[1]Cf. Bertha Phillpotts's reference to the modern convention that 'the author is a kind of god' (page 7 above).

she is (no doubt unconsciously) fishing for a compliment and kow-towing in her own interest to Sir Thomas's patriarchal conservatism. Hence Fanny's embarrassment.

I think Jane Austen's narrative, like the Icelander's, merits the word 'dramatic', but of course it's a different kind of drama, as different as the closed intimate intensities of an Ibsen play are from the open ritualistic movements of a Greek tragedy. Both are dramatic in the sense that a conflict is being acted out in front of an audience or reader and all attention is fixed on the *object or event presented*, whether it's Hallgerd's execution or Fanny's embarrassment.

(ii)   In the sense that she claims to know not only what is spoken in private but what is going on in the minds of her characters (to take up Bertha Phillpotts's point), Jane Austen's stance is indeed 'god-like'. But since Fanny and Edmund (unlike Hallbjorn and Hallgerd) are fictional characters *created* by Jane Austen, this is, on one level at least, inevitable. Within this broad meaning of 'god-like', however, there can be numerous variations: a god can give his creatures more or less freedom and act towards them with varying degrees of arbitrariness. He can also treat his readers with varying degrees of consideration and democracy, either forcing their hand or permitting them the greatest freedom of judgement and interpretation.

Jane Austen, in the passage we're considering, develops her narrative so subtly that it seems unreasonable to accuse her of arbitrariness. In the first paragraph she seems at first, perhaps, to be 'objective' in a rather high-and-mighty god-like way (i.e. claiming a monopoly of truth); but already, though there is no overt irony, there are a number of warning signs. 'Government' is a strong word to use for the authority of the head of a family. 'Sameness and gloom' and 'sombre' must reflect the attitudes not of Sir Thomas himself but of the defeated revellers. In the last two sentences of the paragraph the words 'engagements' and 'solicit' carry, in the circumstances the reader is conscious of, a good deal of weight and ambiguity. After all, we know what kind of people the Rushworths are. The total effect of the first paragraph seems to me very 'open'. While in general it seems to be slanted towards an acceptance of Sir Thomas's point of view, there are so many ambiguities embedded in it that one can't well accuse the author of abusing her power and status by an over-simplification of the issues.

Then come the exchanges between Edmund and Fanny, and they aren't at all simple in their impact. Edmund starts off modestly, limiting his criticism of his father to the socially 'safe' grounds that the Grants do have a 'claim' (a significantly feudal, hierarchical word—closely linked with the important concept of 'gratitude' so often invoked as a positive value in this novel); but it's soon clear that he places a value on the 'liveliness' of the previous period which neither Fanny nor Bertramian orthodoxy can permit. Yet it's Edmund rather than Fanny who keeps the initiative in this conversation and, as we've seen, he scores some palpable hits against what it's kindest to call her timidness or complacency but which really amounts (Jane Austen lets us feel) to a certain complicity with the least satisfactory aspects of the Bertram 'government'. Fanny's tendency, albeit unconsciously, to exploit her role of poor relation is one of the less amiable facets of her character.

What I'm suggesting is that a close examination of the movement of Jane Austen's narrative should lead us to acquit her of the charge of playing god in a pejorative sense. Her 'omniscient' position involves, rather, a poise in which more than one 'point of view' is allowed to develop its force. She sets up a conflict (in this case Edmund's and Fanny's assessment of the situation at Mansfield) and then allows us to watch it develop, as a good dramatist does.

(iii) The underlying point here is that, while Jane Austen's narrative method is (as I've been arguing) 'free' and 'dramatic' (as opposed to being rigidly imposed or crudely manipulated), she does undoubtedly work within a pretty rigid set of basic social—and therefore moral—concepts. Whether this turns out to be an advantage or a disadvantage to her art and status as a novelist is an interesting question. It is possible to argue that the strict social limits within which she operates themselves limit the human relevance of what she is doing; or, on the contrary, that the very precise and specific limitations which she accepts (for don't all artists have to accept *some* such limitation?) give her a remarkable freedom and permit her to establish a poise which is at once tremblingly sensitive and basically secure.

If Jane Austen's narrative stance is 'god-like' it is, I've suggested, that of a god who holds the scales rather than one who arbitrarily imposes his will or 'line'. This is shown by the way the 'point of view' shifts from Edmund to Fanny and back as they discuss their assessments of the situation at Mansfield. In this sense the style and tone of the dialogue reflect the individual discriminations first of one character, then the other. For example, at the end of his first contribution to the dialogue Edmund puts forward the view that the Grants' presence 'would enliven us, and make our evenings pass away with more enjoyment even to my father'. Fanny replies that in her opinion her uncle would not like *any* addition. *She* sees the question entirely in terms of Sir Thomas's wishes, ignoring the possibility that the rest of them might have any independent rights or claims. It is the tension between these two views of the situation—Edmund's and Fanny's—that gives Jane Austen's narrative its vitality at this point, carries the story forward, engages the reader's attention. In this sense the method (essentially dramatic) can be described as depending on the juxtaposing of differing 'attitudes' or 'points of view', involving differing individual moral discriminations.

At the same time it has to be said that the values Edmund and Fanny share are, when all's said and done, more important than those on which they differ. And this is reflected in the unity of tone which Jane Austen does impose on the novel as a whole. Fanny and Edmund may differ in significant discriminations but they do speak very much the same language. Words like 'claim' and 'lively' may be given somewhat different slants but they are used within an agreed set of social assumptions. Fanny's remark that evenings at Mansfield were never merry except when her uncle was in town isn't taken by either of them to imply any sort of criticism or irony. They both accept a view, not just of good manners or social morality but of *the whole nature of personal identity*, which is certainly quite unlike that implied—only thirty years later—by, say, Emily Brontë.

Jane Austen's narrative method—indeed her whole use of language—seems to me to depend at a very basic level on her acceptance of certain stable social values which (she can assume) are shared (either in actual practice or through an imaginative understanding) by her readers. In this sense her method is not really so very different from the old saga-teller's, even though she is operating in a far more sophisticated context. The judgements on Maria and Mrs Norris at the end of *Mansfield Park* are not, I think, any more ambiguous than the treatment of Hallgerd in the Icelandic narrative. Both Sir Thomas and Hallbjorn act within the prescribed conception of their rights and duties, and though they are not unfeeling we have no reason to suppose they have any very fundamental moral qualms or psychological conflicts. If Jane Austen's narrative stance is more god-like it is so only in the sense that a somewhat greater flexibility of individual discrimination was permissible in late eighteenth-century upper-class English society than in tenth-century Iceland. Isn't 'the watching countryside' (or at least the genteel section of the countryside) almost as much a factor in a Jane Austen novel as in the story of Hallbjorn and Hallgerd?

3 George Eliot

This passage is from *Middlemarch* (Penguin ed., pp. 401–02) and is an extract from a scene between Dorothea and Will Ladislaw in which the latter is telling about his parents and grandparents and the nature of their relationship with the Casaubon family. (You'll recall that Will's grandmother, 'Aunt Julia'—Mr Casaubon's mother's sister—had been disinherited by the Casaubons on account of a misalliance with a Polish refugee and that Mr Casaubon himself had later accepted responsibility for Will and his mother.) I have chosen a passage involving conversation to make comparison with the last passage more valid, but it's worth remembering that in *Middlemarch* much of the narrative involves not conversation but the descriptive analysis of the feelings of particular characters.

Dorothea is asking Will about the past when the passage opens:

> '. . . But tell me how it was—Mr Casaubon could not have known about you then.'

> 'No; but my father had made himself known to Mr Casaubon, and that was my last hungry day. My father died soon after, and my mother and I were well taken care of. Mr Casaubon always expressly recognized it as his duty to take care of us because of the harsh injustice which had been shown to his mother's sister. But now I am telling you what is not new to you.'

> In his inmost soul Will was conscious of wishing to tell Dorothea what was rather new even in his own construction of things—namely, that Mr Casaubon had never done more than pay a debt towards him. Will was much too good a fellow to be easy under the sense of being ungrateful. And when gratitude has become a matter of reasoning there are many ways of escaping from its bonds.

> 'No,' answered Dorothea; 'Mr Casaubon has always avoided dwelling on his honourable actions.' She did not feel that her husband's conduct was depreciated; but this notion of what justice had required in his relations with Will Ladislaw took strong hold on her mind. After a moment's pause, she added, 'He had never told me that he supported your mother. Is she still living?'

> 'No; she died by an accident—a fall—four years ago. It is curious that my mother, too, ran away from her family, but not for the sake of a husband. She never would tell me anything about her family, except that she forsook them to get her own living—went on the stage, in fact. She was a dark-eyed creature, with crisp ringlets, and never seemed to be getting old. You see I come of rebellious blood on both sides,' Will ended, smiling brightly at Dorothea, while she was still looking with serious intentness before her, like a child seeing a drama for the first time.

> But her face, too, broke into a smile as she said, 'That is your apology, I suppose, for having yourself been rather rebellious; I mean, to Mr Casaubon's wishes. You must remember that you have not done what he thought best for you. And if he dislikes you—you were speaking of dislike a little while ago—but I should rather say, if he has shown any painful feelings towards you, you must consider how sensitive he has become from the wearing effect of study. Perhaps,' she continued, getting into a pleading tone, 'my uncle has not told you how serious Mr

Casaubon's illness was. It would be petty of us who are well and can bear things, to think much of small offences from those who carry a weight of trial.'

'You teach me better,' said Will. 'I will never grumble on that subject again.' There was a gentleness in his tone which came from the unutterable contentment of perceiving—what Dorothea was hardly conscious of—that she was travelling into the remoteness of pure pity and loyalty towards her husband. Will was ready to adore her pity and loyalty, if she would associate himself with her in manifesting them. 'I have really sometimes been a perverse fellow,' he went on, 'but I will never again, if I can help it, do or say what you would disapprove.'

'That is very good of you,' said Dorothea, with another open smile. 'I shall have a little kingdom then, where I shall give laws . . .'

When you have read the passage carefully, make notes on the following topic: in what ways does George Eliot's way of telling her story seem to differ from Jane Austen's? What are the implications of these differences as far as the basic aims and artistic attitudes of the two novelists are concerned?

Discussion

George Eliot's tone in this scene (and I think it's fairly typical) seems to me a good deal less intimate than Jane Austen's, despite the former's habit of giving us glimpses into her characters' 'inmost soul' or unspoken thoughts. Of course this is *partly* due to the fact that Dorothea's relationship with Ladislaw is at this stage much less intimate than Fanny's with Edmund (though by coincidence both couples are cousins of some sort[1]); but I don't think it's simply that. Doesn't Jane Austen stand *in general* in a closer relationship towards her people than George Eliot? My impression is that one always gets the sense of Jane Austen's closeness and critical participation in the scenes she describes. In comparison George Eliot's narrative stance seems much more distant and aloof—god-like in that sense, perhaps.

This sense of distance I am emphasizing has nothing to do with George Eliot's sympathy for her characters, which is in some respects more inclusive (more conscientious, one might almost say) than Jane Austen's. I associate it rather with a more analytical cast of mind, a less unified social context, and perhaps the fact that as a national, and even international, intellectual figure her way of life was very different from her predecessor's. She cannot use words or appeal to responses as securely based as Jane Austen's. Take, for example, the way the words 'ungrateful' and 'gratitude' are used in this passage. For George Eliot and her characters the claims of 'gratitude' have become altogether more complex and problematical than for anyone in *Mansfield Park*. Will Ladislaw isn't at all sure that he need be grateful to Mr Casaubon for supporting his mother and himself. Words like 'pity' and 'loyalty' near the end of the passage are, again, used with an acute sense of their problematical nature. This is, above all, a matter of changing social developments and values. George Eliot doesn't *share* the values of Middlemarch in quite the way Jane Austen seems to share those of Mansfield Park.[2] Nor can she be so sure that her readers will react in the same way. For these reasons abstract nouns like 'gratitude' and 'loyalty' can't be used by her with the same sort of

[1]And, interestingly, Ladislaw is a 'poor relation'.

[2]This may be partly because the story is set in the past: but it may also be *why* it's set in the past.

confidence in their meaning. Her narrative has to pause, so to speak, while the various possible moral implications of such words are considered.

The two paragraphs beginning 'In his inmost soul' and ' "No," answered Dorothea' illustrate the point. In both cases (the one describing Will, the other Dorothea) George Eliot takes it upon herself to 'explain', in ways that they themselves are scarcely capable of, the operation of her characters' minds. In recording Dorothea's remark about her husband she permits herself a kind of irony which depends for its operation on our (the readers') being more aware of the situation than is Dorothea herself. Now Jane Austen will use this trick with minor and unsympathetic characters (Mrs Norris, for instance) but I don't think she would do it with Fanny or any of her main characters. You might say that this is because Jane Austen avoids seeming to take advantage of her own people; but it's also connected with the 'closed' social area within which she works. George Eliot's assumption of the more obviously 'omniscient' role comes at least partly from the fact that she is operating in a more complex and wider social situation, in which—because there is no longer a general acceptance of a single social ethos—she is *forced* to assume a more god-like role and to define her own basis of operations. To put it a bit crudely: Jane Austen has no need to tell us what is in Edmund's inmost soul, since we are able, within that stable order, to know it from his role and actions; but George Eliot can't bring Dorothea and Ladislaw into contact without using a number of asides and authorial insights to explain their thoughts and motives. What is behind George Eliot's phrase 'In his inmost soul Will was conscious . . .' etc. is that there is a deep cleavage between the conventional moral assessments involved in Dorothea's assumptions about Mr Casaubon and Will's own assessment of the situation. Because Will can no longer accept Casaubon's moral standards he finds it difficult to communicate with Dorothea, who can. It is as though Edmund, in his conversation with Fanny, had suddenly begun questioning the basic validity of the Mansfield ethos. But this is not a possibility Jane Austen contemplates. She can still appeal to 'the watching countryside'. George Eliot's audience, as well as the society she is describing, is less homogeneous.[1] Hence her feeling that, to make sure her reader 'understands' what is happening, she must guide his reactions more overtly and claim insights which 'any intelligent person in the countryside' may not necessarily be able to infer for himself.

It seems to me that in the last complete paragraph of our passage (the one beginning 'You teach me better . . .') George Eliot falls—and it's not a sudden change of tactics—into a mode of narration quite different from the one Jane Austen, let alone the saga-teller, adopts. Not only is she taking the reader further into the minds of her characters than her predecessors would have done, she is doing it not by revealing their feelings in action but by describing them. And this involves a new sort of covenant between author and reader: the novelist treats her reader with a sort of complicity. Together they know more than either of the characters being presented, so that author and reader can share a superiority (which expresses itself in irony). Jane Austen's irony doesn't, I think, involve this sort of exclusiveness. You don't have to be a special sort of person to recognize that Lady Bertram is absurd. Jane Austen may operate within a narrow and exclusive world—a 'closed' world, socially—but within it attitudes and ethics are *shared* and therefore 'open' in the sense that the saga-teller's narrative is 'open'. George Eliot's narrative stance, her 'point of view', seems to me to involve a somewhat different relationship both to her material and to her reader. If I say she is *superior* to her material and is out to involve the reader in her own superior sensibility, that sounds unsympathetic, which I don't mean it to. Yet I can't find a better

[1] And, incidentally, more urban, with all the social and psychological changes that involves.

14

word. George Eliot is, I can't help feeling, a very superior person, with *all* that that implies. The shift from Jane Austen's sort of narrative to George Eliot's is linked, I think, with large social and intellectual developments for which neither writer can be held responsible. On the one hand, the range of human activity and experience which the later novelist covers is much wider and more complex; on the other hand, the novelist has withdrawn from the midst of things to an increasingly special vantage-point. You can describe this vantage-point in terms of art or ideology or social relationship. It is 'special' in the sense that George Eliot and Henry James are—and that Jane Austen and Emily Brontë and Dickens and Hardy aren't—in some way or other 'outside' the world they create and convey.

This isn't an easy question and needs plenty of thought. In one sense, of course, *all* artists are outside their work—the creator is by definition bound to stand outside his creation. In another sense *no* artist can possibly stand altogether or entirely outside the world (or his creation), for what he knows and feels and can create is in the nature of things limited by the world, for there is nothing else. So the question I am discussing (the relationship of the novelist to his work and public) is a narrower and more specialized one than these big general questions. It boils down to a matter of defining the sense in which a writer like George Eliot—highly morally and socially responsible, conscientiously modest, immensely conscious of her duties to her created characters as well as to the world at large—makes a special claim with regard to her relationship to her characters, and perhaps to life in general. To define at all adequately George Eliot's relationship to Dorothea and Ladislaw in our passage would involve, I think, defining her attitude and relationship to Middlemarch itself and, indeed, to mid-nineteenth-century English society. This is a more complex question than that of Jane Austen's relationship to *her* society, or the saga-teller's to his, and the complexity isn't just a matter of technological development: it involves questions of class and the changing role of the intellectual in a bourgeois-democratic society. In discussing the 'god-like' stance of George Eliot the novelist it is highly relevant to recall that the mid-nineteenth-century intellectual was a very special kind of god. I shall have a bit more to say on this question in Section 2 of this unit; and you will find it picked up again by John Goode in Section 5.

4 Henry James

The passage this time is from the very end of *What Maisie Knew* and would be quite incomprehensible to anyone who hadn't read the novel. The four characters, Maisie, Mrs Wix, Mrs Beale and Sir Claude, are in Boulogne in the hotel where they have been staying. Maisie and Sir Claude have just come from the station, where Maisie has reached her momentous decision: she will 'give up' Mrs Wix only if Sir Claude will 'give up' Mrs Beale (Penguin ed., pp. 247–48):

> They stood confronted, the step-parents, still under Maisie's observation. That observation had never sunk so deep as at this particular moment. 'Yes, my dear, I haven't given you up,' Sir Claude said to Mrs Beale at last, 'and if you'd like me to treat our friends here as solemn witnesses I don't mind giving you my word for it that I never will. There!' he dauntlessly exclaimed.
>
> 'He can't!' Mrs Wix tragically commented.
>
> Mrs Beale, erect and alive in her defeat, jerked her handsome face about. 'He can't!' she literally mocked.
>
> 'He can't, he can't, he can't!'—Sir Claude's gay emphasis wonderfully carried it off.

Mrs Beale took it all in, yet she held her ground; on which Maisie addressed Mrs Wix. 'Shan't we lose the boat?'

'Yes, we shall lose the boat,' Mrs Wix remarked to Sir Claude.

Mrs Beale meanwhile faced full at Maisie. 'I don't know what to make of you!' she launched.

'Good-bye,' said Maisie to Sir Claude.

'Good-bye, Maisie,' Sir Claude answered.

Mrs Beale came away from the door. 'Good-bye!' she hurled at Maisie; then passed straight across the room and disappeared in the adjoining one.

Sir Claude had reached the other door and opened it. Mrs Wix was already out. On the threshold Maisie paused; she put out her hand to her stepfather. He took it and held it a moment, and their eyes met as the eyes of those who have done for each other what they can. 'Good-bye,' he repeated.

'Good-bye.' And Maisie followed Mrs Wix.

They caught the steamer, which was just putting off, and, hustled across the gulf, found themselves on the deck so breathless and so scared that they gave up half the voyage to letting their emotion sink. It sank slowly and imperfectly; but at last, in mid-channel, surrounded by the quiet sea, Mrs Wix had courage to revert. 'I didn't look back, did you?'

'Yes. He wasn't there,' said Maisie.

'Not on the balcony?'

Maisie waited a moment; then 'He wasn't there' she simply said again.

Mrs Wix was also silent a while. 'He went to *her*,' she finally observed.

'Oh I know!' the child replied.

Mrs Wix gave a sidelong look. She still had room for wonder at what Maisie knew.

Your exercise is to consider the passage in the light of the issues we have been discussing. Try to analyse James's narrative method and to describe his own stance or point of view. Consider words like 'dramatic', 'descriptive', 'omniscient' in relation to the passage. How does it compare with the previous passages?

Discussion

We have to say first, I think, that James's method is, like passages 1 and 2 and to a greater extent than passage 3, overtly 'dramatic', i.e. the scenes 'act themselves out' before us. We *watch* what is happening and are not merely told about it by someone else. James, like Jane Austen, always keeps our eye on the object and directs our attention away from himself.

It's true, of course, that the scene isn't *pure* drama, i.e. without any sort of exterior comment. James underlines a number of points which his reader couldn't necessarily be expected to infer from the dialogue itself. We are *told* (as opposed to shown) that Maisie's 'observation' had never before 'sunk so deep'. Mrs Beale's 'defeat' is stressed. The final glance between Maisie and Sir Claude is described; so is the condition of Maisie and Mrs Wix (breathless and scared) as they settle down on the boat they have so nearly missed. Yet these descriptive touches, and the use of a word like 'launched' in place of the more neutral 'said', really perform the function of 'stage directions' rather than non-dramatic 'description'. They offer to the reader the sort of hints which stage directions offer the actors in a drama.

But it is, of course, a funny kind of drama, because there is so much room for speculation—on one level at least—as to what is actually happening. The actual words of the dialogue tell us extremely little (try reading them separately, divorced from the directing 'instructions' James so subtly offers). Everything depends on the tone of voice and implication. (Perhaps this is why James's novels turn out to be so unexpectedly effective when well adapted to television.)

Individual descriptive words are all-important in James's method. Notice, in the first third of our passage, the force of the adverbs 'dauntlessly', 'tragically', 'literally', 'wonderfully'. They are really what colour the passage, I think, and the odd thing about them, again, is that they are so ambiguous, used (except perhaps 'literally') with several layers of irony to them—for Sir Claude isn't really at all dauntless and only in a very special, Jamesian sense 'wonderful' (which seems to mean something like 'expressive': James often seems to use the word to indicate that his characters are serving his purposes admirably), and Mrs Wix's tragic poses are at the same time comic.

The tension between his dramatic method and the highly individual, ambiguous tone is what gives a Henry James novel its peculiar effect. With the one hand he presents a scene, a conflict, with great clarity and precision; with the other he dissipates the effect and forces us to look again. Take the word 'wonder' in the final sentence of the book. Does it imply uncertainty (I wonder how much she knows) or an awed admiration (I wonder at how much she knows)? Readers who don't enjoy Henry James often complain of the excess of art in his productions: he himself would have said that without art nothing is interesting and that to complain about the way he uses language is like complaining about the poetry of a poem.

Another way of putting the same paradox is that if James, among our novelists, is the one most conscious of his art, he is also the one most concerned to conceal his art. This is why, like Maisie herself, he cannot avoid a question which I don't think any other novel in this course is likely to elicit: may not the whole thing be, perhaps, an extraordinary example of sleight of hand? An artist as self-consciously enigmatic as James can scarcely complain if his reader finds himself asking whether the sphinx really has a secret.

I have called his method dramatic (which is to imply that he abjures straightforward description); but it would be entirely wrong to link it directly with the method of the saga-teller. For one thing, James, like Jane Austen, is concerned with discriminations which cannot be revealed by actions alone; for another, there is no longer a trace of the watching countryside. The readership for which *Maisie* is designed is socially sophisticated and morally 'open'; urbane in every sense. That reader must be prepared continuously to question his own assumptions, to accept indeed a presumption which neither Jane Austen nor George Eliot (let alone the saga-teller) could well have stomached, that is to say that Maisie's moral consciousness flourishes in inverse proportion to the corruption which she encounters. The sentence that describes the parting of Maisie and Sir Claude ('their eyes met as the eyes of those who have done for each other what they can') is about as worldly a sentence as you will find in a nineteenth-century novel, yet it commits the writer to nothing. What these two have done for one another is left entirely for the reader to decide. The moral implications of Maisie's decision (which all James's resources go to assure us is 'wonderful') are not discussed or, in any usual sense, articulated, though I think they are *conveyed* through James's highly elliptical use of language.

Any sort of analysis of even a short passage of *What Maisie Knew* seems to me to lead one straight to the central dilemma of this particular novel. Can we accept Maisie or, perhaps one should say, Maisie's innocence? Since, with James, moral and aesthetic values are so closely identified, the question is not an abstract one. If *Maisie* 'comes off' as a novel, James's claims for its moral insights are automatically assured. If the central 'light vessel of consciousness' is in any important sense a blank, then it's hard for the reader to avoid a sense of being led up the garden.

Is the narrative stance of Henry James more or less 'god-like' than, say, George Eliot's? It depends, I think, on the sort of attributes you stress in the two novelists and how you define your terms. In one sense James keeps a tighter rein over his material than George Eliot: every move in his game is worked out with the greatest possible care, nothing left to chance. Yet he would scorn to reveal his hand, to deliver *ex cathedra* judgements about his people in the way George Eliot sometimes does. This doesn't mean, obviously, that he is less concerned than George Eliot to 'direct' our responses; rather that he articulates his 'directions' in a different way, perhaps inevitably, for they are of a different kind. The key word in the final chapter of *Maisie* (it comes before our passage) is, I think, 'right'.

> 'She made her condition [Sir Claude says of Maisie] with such a sense of what it should be! She made the only right one.'
> 'The only right one?'—Mrs Beale returned to the charge. (page 244)

If we compare what Henry James means by the word 'right' with what the word implies to Jane Austen or George Eliot, we come near, I think, to suggesting the difference between his narrative method *and* his 'point of view' and those of either of them. 'Right' has a consciously 'aesthetic' dimension for Henry James. When he refers to Maisie's choice as being 'right' he is using the word in the way that a painter or a musician does when he is trying to find the 'right' way of finishing his painting or his sonata. He does not abstract the 'moral' from the 'art' but assumes that the two are, if not identical, interdependent. But he *thinks*, or operates, or works (or whatever word one best uses to describe what an artist *does*) in terms of 'art' and its language. Whereas what is 'right' for Fanny or for Dorothea is thought of in terms more easily related to the more common language of moral or ethical discourse. (Note: I am *not* suggesting that Henry James isn't interested in morality or that Jane Austen and George Eliot aren't interested in art: the distinction I'm making is much less absolute than that.)

A note on 'Narrate or describe'

Lukács, in the essay 'Narrate or describe?' in the Course Reader (pp. 62ff.), contrasts the methods of Tolstoy and Zola. Tolstoy 'narrates', Zola 'describes'. Of course Lukács doesn't claim that the distinction is absolute: 'There are no writers who renounce description absolutely. Nor . . . can one claim that the outstanding representatives of realism after 1848, Flaubert and Zola, renounced narration absolutely.' Nevertheless, he sees a *tendency* to move from a reliance on narration to a predominance of description as a significant development in the nineteenth-century novel and he relates it to a movement away from 'experiencing' towards 'observing' and says that this 'arises out of divergent basic positions about life and about the major problems of society and not just out of divergent artistic methods . . .'

We don't have time for a full discussion of Lukács's thesis[1] and my aim is

[1]I have already stressed that my own use of the term 'narrative' is broader than his: 'narrate' and 'describe' are, in my sense, alternative narrative methods.

simply to consider *Germinal* very briefly in the light of it. But those of you who want to pursue this question had better first make sure that you have fully understood the distinction between 'narration' and 'description' on which the argument (irrespective of its validity) is based.

So first pick out from Lukács's essay sentences which seem to you to define his meaning of (a) narration, and (b) description.

Discussion

(a)   Narration (Lukács says) is what Tolstoy achieves when he presents the horse-race in *Anna Karenina* from 'the standpoint of a participant'. In narration 'We are the audience to events in which the characters take active part. We ourselves experience these events.' Narration is essentially 'dramatic', involving an emphasis on the object or situation.

(b)   Description is what characterizes the methods of Flaubert and Zola and becomes more common in fiction after the middle of the nineteenth century. It implies 'telling' the reader about something rather than allowing him to 'experience' it, and Lukács associates it with 'observing' as opposed to 'experiencing' and with 'levelling' as opposed to a maintenance of 'proportion'.

I think it is fair to say that Lukács is dealing with 'trends' or 'tendencies' rather than attempting to characterize the work of particular novelists (though he is apt to fall into the latter activity) and also that he is more concerned with the total effect of a book than with detailed stylistic or formal analysis. When he goes in for the latter it is to illustrate a general point he wishes to make rather than to use it methodologically as a starting-point for his assessment of a novelist's basic 'point of view'. He is suspicious of empiricism, seeing it as tending to stress arbitrary, subjective or superficial factors rather than essential ones, the essential thing being the relationship of the writer to his material and to his audience, the *way* he sees the world, which determines *what* he sees.

I want to discuss one particular problem arising out of Lukács's argument. If 'narration' (in the sense Lukács uses the term) is the essential key to the novelist's art, the art that produces what Lawrence would call a 'tremulation' that 'can make the whole man alive tremble', how are we to account for the power of a novel like *Germinal* to move us?

If we compare *Germinal* with *Cousin Bette* we are bound to see, I think, the force of Lukács's distinction between 'description' and 'narration'. In *Cousin Bette* everything is 'dramatic', 'acted out'. It's true that Balzac includes longish passages of description, as well as all manner of moral asides, and that his style is full of his personal mannerisms; but these are not the core of the book, they are absorbed into it and have the effect of adding to its 'body' rather than detracting from it. The core of the book is the central situation acted out before us by the conflicting characters. It's they who 'live' and they live through the intensity of their relationships with one another and the monstrous force of the characteristics generated in them by these relationships. Lukács is quite right when he stresses 'the dramatic element' in Balzac and goes on to say:

> Balzac's extraordinarily multi-faceted, complicated characterizations could not possibly emerge with such impressive dramatic effectiveness if the environmental conditions in their lives were not depicted in such breadth. (page 69)

It is also true that Zola, both in theory and practice, works differently. It's interesting to see *his* description of what he thinks is Balzac's method in *Cousin Bette*:

> The novelist starts out in search of a truth. I will take as an example the character of the Baron Hulot, in *Cousine Bette*, by Balzac. The general fact observed by Balzac is the ravages that the amorous temperament of a man makes in his home, in his family, and in society. As soon as he has chosen his subject he starts from known facts; then he makes his experiment, and exposes Hulot to a series of trials, placing him amid certain surroundings in order to exhibit how the complicated machinery of his passions works. It is then evident that there is not only observation there, but that there is also experiment; as Balzac does not remain satisfied with photographing the facts collected by him, but interferes in a direct way to place his character in certain conditions, and of these he remains the master. The problem is to know what such a passion, acting in such a surrounding and under such circumstances, would produce from the point of view of an individual and of society; and an experimental novel, *Cousine Bette*, for example, is simply the report of the experiment that the novelist conducts before the eyes of the public. In fact, the whole operation consists in taking facts in nature, then in studying the mechanism of these facts, acting upon them, by the modification of circumstances and surroundings, without deviating from the laws of nature. Finally, you possess knowledge of the man, scientific knowledge of him, in both his individual and social relations. (Course Reader, pp. 296–97)

This seems to me a most significant passage and one which merits more consideration than we have time to give it. In some ways Zola's 'experimental method' offers excellent insights into Balzac's mode of operation: his description of Balzac making 'his experiment' and 'exposing Hulot to a series of trials' is a good way of pin-pointing the 'dramatic' method of *Cousin Bette*. 'Observation' and 'experiment' in this passage correspond closely to the Lukács categories of 'describe' and 'narrate'. Where Zola is much less near the mark is in his analysis of the 'creation' of Baron Hulot. He seems to see this in terms of the gathering of observed facts about an isolated individual or type. But surely the point about Balzac's presentation of the Baron is that he *doesn't* see him simply as the type of an 'amorous' temperament. On the contrary, he presents him always as part of a dramatically conceived situation which involves Bette, Adeline, Crevel and Mme Marneffe (to mention only the most important figures) and, beyond them, the whole history of French society from the Revolution to 1846. If Baron Hulot is a type, his 'typicality' is embedded in a total situation, family and social, and it is precisely this that allows Balzac to develop a method which is 'dramatic' and humanly vibrant, rather than 'descriptive', 'experimental' and humanly flat.

I don't think *Germinal* can be dismissed as 'flat' but I do think there are elements of flatness in it that come from Zola's method, which, in contrast to Balzac's, doesn't give his characters their head or indeed present them as vibrant human beings achieving their vitality (for better or worse) through their dramatic inter-relationship with one another. The drama of *Germinal* is the drama of conflicting 'forces' rather than a drama expressed through a concentration on relationships which are, as in Balzac, both personal *and* social. The role of Étienne in the novel underlines this. He comes to Village 240 at the beginning and goes away at the end. It isn't adequate to call him an observer, because in fact he participates actively in the situation he finds; but, given the degree to which events involve him in the life of the community, it's an oddly limited participation. His relationship with Catherine is not *un*-convincing; but it isn't deeply realized. To me the only relationship he enters into that is realized on a humanly 'vibrant' level is with Maheude, and I find their final conversation moving because it expresses poignantly the fact that they *might* have had a closer relationship. This episode 'places' Étienne in relation to the community and to the novel as a whole and explains why his role is at bottom that of observer rather than participant, not just in terms of the story, but *artistically*. By choosing to present his novel so much *through* Étienne, Zola in effect prevented the possibility of a fully 'dramatic' realization of the conflicts he uncovers. It is rather as though Balzac had given Victorin Hulot, who is never *totally* involved in the drama, a key role in the structure of *Cousin Bette*.

Étienne's role in *Germinal* isn't, of course, an accident. It is an attempt by Zola to bridge the gap which, as John Berger puts it (in Television Programme 11), inevitably existed between his own experience as a writer and the experience of the miners that is the subject of the novel. It's not hard to see why the narrative method of *Germinal* should have been (quite apart from the theory of naturalism) descriptive rather than dramatic. What is more difficult to explain is how, given these circumstances, *Germinal* turns out to be an impressive novel. Berger proposes one possible explanation in his programme. Brian Nicholas has offered a different one, speculating that the naturalistic theory was particularly fruitful in relation to the novels of working-class life of this period because, with its deterministic emphasis, it was well adapted to books about the hopelessness of the predicament of working-class people faced with a situation (and social and economic forces) which they were unable to control or defeat. Another argument that has sometimes been used is that the novel of industrial society is bound to put more stress on groups and 'forces' than on individuals who are themselves in no real sense free agents within that society.

These last two suggestions are perhaps more successful in *explaining Germinal* than in evaluating it. It's to be hoped that you will give the problem some thought and try to decide for yourself what it is that's so impressive about *Germinal* and what implications that impressiveness has.

2   *The good and the popular*

(By Arnold Kettle)

Right through the nineteenth century it was assumed or agreed that, despite the great merits of Jane Austen and the Brontës, the two great British novelists of the early decades of the century were Scott and Dickens. There was also Thackeray, who, by the mid-century, was often bracketed with Dickens; but that was a little later. The first big figures were Scott and Dickens: big in achievement, big in influence, big in fame. And they were also—it's somehow an integral part of their stature—the big sellers, the popular novelists who lifted circulation figures to a new height.

Of course, as we saw in Unit 11, the situation wasn't quite as simple as that account suggests. Circulations were still comparatively limited and the social basis of the readership, especially of Scott, was still fairly narrow: it was only with serialization and later 'cheap editions' (still costing, however, upwards of two or three shillings) that this changed. Our picture also plays down the importance of the 'penny issue' publications of the 1830s onwards. Nevertheless, the fact remains: the two great novelists were also the two popular novelists. Whatever reservations he might have about the bad effects of trashy novels, it would scarcely have occurred to the intelligent observer of the literary scene in the 1840s to hold that the 'good' and the 'popular' were opposites and probably irreconcilable.

By the end of the century the situation was different. George Eliot and Thomas Hardy were well-known writers, comparatively widely read; but their names (and even less Henry James's) would not be found on a list of best-sellers of the last decades. On the contrary, the names that would immediately have asserted themselves were Mrs Henry Wood and Marie Corelli, heading a list which would include Charlotte Mary Yonge, Miss Braddon and Ouida. *Lady Audley's Secret*, *East Lynne* and *The Sorrows of Satan* are the relevant titles rather than *Middlemarch*, *What Maisie Knew* or *Tess of the d'Urbervilles*. That, of course, isn't the whole story either. The rise of the 'queens of the circulating libraries' was only one sort of phenomenon in the development of the popular fiction of the day, and a predominantly middle-class one, even though their readership certainly extended 'below stairs'. And even larger circulations were to be found among the producers of cheaper, more obviously unrespectable literature.

The reasons for the change—the increasing separation of the 'good' and the 'popular'—aren't difficult to see and you should be able to jot them down without much mental exertion.

Discussion

(i)   The extension of literacy. (By the end of the century almost everyone was 'officially' literate.)

(ii)   The numerical growth of a comfortable, prosperous, leisured middle-class reading public.

(iii)   The continued existence of 'two worlds'—the rich and the poor—with a minimum of contact with each other.

(iv)   The continued rise of commercial publishing on a mass scale as an immensely profitable business.

It's worth, perhaps, making two additional general points:

(a)   The extension of literacy doesn't automatically produce a divided public. It is, however, likely to do so if it is accompanied by great social inequality, a minimal system of education and a 'market' economy in which publishing becomes a commercial business.

(b)   A more refined and detailed answer would, of course, have to examine such questions as the ideological role of the novel in spreading and propagandizing certain ideas, attitudes and values—moral, social, religious, economic—as opposed to others. It would be very naïve to underestimate the value of fiction to its purveyors not only as a source of income but as a means of 'keeping people happy', with all that that implies.

We can't possibly, however, in the time at our disposal, go into the general sociological and cultural problems involved in the development of large-scale commercial publishing and the mass media. This section has a more limited aim. What we need to consider, if we are to think fruitfully about the achievements of the great nineteenth-century novelists, are some of the main implications *for the novelists themselves* of the widening gap between the 'good' and the 'popular'.

The problem is well illustrated by some remarks of George Eliot (from *Theophrastus Such*, 1879):

For a man who has a certain gift of writing to say, 'I will make the most of it while the public likes my wares—as long as the market is open and I am able to supply it at a money profit—such profit being the sign of liking'—he should have a belief that his wares have nothing akin to the arsenic green in them, and also that his continuous supply is secure from a degradation in quality which the habit of consumption encouraged in the buyers may hinder them from marking their sense of by rejection; so that they complain, but pay, and read while they complain. Unless he has that belief, he is on a level with the manufacturer who gets rich by fancy-wares coloured with arsenic green. He really cares for nothing but his income. He carries on authorship on the principle of the gin-palace.

And bad literature of the sort called amusing is spiritual gin. (Quoted in Miriam Allott (ed.), *Novelists on the Novel*, page 94)

It's worth comparing this passage with the remarks of Dickens's friend Wilkie Collins made only twenty years earlier (and quoted in part in Unit 11):

The future of English fiction may rest with this Unknown Public, which is now waiting to be taught the difference between a good book and a bad . . . It is probably a question of time only. The largest audience for periodical literature, in this age of periodicals, must obey the universal law of progress, and must, sooner or later, learn to discriminate. When that period comes, the readers who rank by millions will be the readers who give the widest reputations, who return the richest rewards, and who will, therefore, command the services of the best writers of their time. A great, an unparalleled prospect awaits, perhaps, the coming generation of English novelists. To the penny journals of the present time belongs the credit of having discovered a new public. When the public shall discover its need of a great writer, the great writer will have such an audience as has never yet been known. (*Household Words*, xviii, 1858, pp. 217–24)

How would you contrast these two passages? What attitude to the novelist's relation to his public do they imply?

Discussion

The obvious contrast is that while Collins was optimistic about the situation produced by the growth of commercial publishing, George Eliot is pessimistic. Collins, in 1858, saw the extension of the reading public as an invigorating challenge to the novelist which could bring about a more valuable, more universal sort of literature; George Eliot, by 1879, sees it as a danger, a form of corruption. Of course, not every writer in the 'fifties was as optimistic as Collins, nor everyone by 1879 as full of foreboding as George Eliot; yet their contrasting attitudes are historically significant.

The danger of authorship being carried on on 'the principle of the gin-palace' appalled George Eliot. It's hard to imagine Jane Austen, Emily Brontë or Dickens expressing such a sentiment. For neither of the first two (for both historical and personal reasons) was the development of the reading public or the growth of commercial publishing much of an issue. For Dickens they were certainly issues, but ones which like, Wilkie Collins, he met with confidence, though not without qualms.[1] The point is not that the earlier novelists were

[1]Students interested in Dickens's attitude to the novel are referred to Richard Stang, *The Theory of the Novel in England, 1850–1870*. Stang sums up Dickens's attitudes: 'Dickens' view was always that the novelist should address the entire literate nation, and the great writer must be a popular writer' (page 22); and 'Dickens never believed he created microcosms of the society for their own sake or their own intrinsic beauty. They were given to his reader so that he could understand his world and so change it' (page 28).

unaware of the dangers of bad or trivial or escapist literature (*Northanger Abbey* makes Jane Austen's attitude clear), but rather that *they did not look upon the general cultural developments of the day as inherently inimical to their role as writers*.

What lies behind George Eliot's fear of bad literature as spiritual gin is not simply a suspicion of commercialism. A shift in the whole way that a novelist should see his role and his art is involved. George Eliot and Henry James both had serious reservations about Dickens's art and tended to consider him, though no doubt some sort of natural genius, both superficial and vulgar.[1] For all his vitality, he didn't quite qualify as 'serious'. This view of Dickens (and it was a very common one amongst novelists and critics right up to the Second World War) links up with a withdrawal from the very idea of 'popular literature'.

George Eliot took her responsibilities as a novelist every bit as seriously as Dickens had done: she believed as much as he did that the novel had a social and moral mission, and went even further, talking of 'the sacredness of the writer's art' (*Westminster Review*, LXIV, page 460). This shift is significant. She talks much more about 'art' than Dickens does and much less about changing or reforming things. And her tone is different. Whereas Dickens spoke directly to his public through the idiom of a popular culture he had absorbed and used, George Eliot is more aloof, more superior, and, I think one must say, much more middle-class.

This difference of tone reflects a difference in her conception of her role. For all her emphasis on moral decision, she is much more chary than Dickens about the elements of straight didacticism which he (with his not infrequent appeals to the public conscience) is able to absorb into his novels.

> I think aesthetic teaching is the highest of all teaching because it deals with life in its highest complexity. But if it ceases to be purely aesthetic . . . it becomes the most offensive of all teaching. (*The George Eliot Letters*, vol. IV, page 300)

It is interesting to note that this is the moment at which a strong suspicion of didacticism—which such novelists as Defoe, Fielding, Richardson, Scott and Dickens had all frankly absorbed into their work—first arises. Artistic purpose is much less down-to-earth for George Eliot than for her predecessors. To justify her sacred office she has to develop a theory of art and moral responsibility of a much more generalized kind than Dickens's. Art has to 'enlarge men's sympathies':

> If Art does not enlarge men's sympathies, it does nothing morally . . . The only effect I ardently long to produce by my writings, is that those who read them should be better able to *imagine* and to *feel* the pains and the joys of those who differ from themselves in everything but the broad fact of being struggling, erring human creatures. (Ibid., loc. cit.)[2]

It's not so much that Dickens would have *disagreed* with these last statements, as that he would not have felt the need to make them. Indeed, he would probably have felt a certain suspicion about the whole process of generalizing about human life and art in this way. An emotion which permeates *Great Expectations*, but is much less evident in *Middlemarch* or *What Maisie Knew*, is

---

[1]G. H. Lewes, with whom she lived, went much further than George Eliot, complaining of 'the pervading commonness' of his novels.

[2]The argument is comparable to that of Shelley in *The Defence of Poetry*, though Shelley would scarcely have used the word 'erring' in the same spirit.

indignation. 'Art' as conceived by George Eliot and Henry James tends to replace indignation by compassion and in the process the meaning of the word 'sympathy' is subtly changed. George Eliot, I'm suggesting, in order to bring herself into touch with the mass of humanity whom she genuinely wishes (wise, compassionate and humane as she is) to serve, has first to do something Dickens did not feel the need to do: to establish for herself a *special* position, a special stance as a creator, the stance of the morally responsible artist, uncorrupted by commercial pressures or by the vulgarity of didacticism, and therefore in an essential sense above and outside the actual struggles in which not only Dickens but, in their own worlds, Jane Austen and Emily Brontë had participated. Fear of 'commonness' is a very deep fear in George Eliot's sensibility, and though it isn't fair to interpret it in purely social (still less in snobbish) terms, it certainly isn't without its social ramifications.

Henry James goes further than George Eliot. For him Art is everything. 'It is art that *makes* life . . .,' he was to write to H. G. Wells. What James meant by art isn't something that can be identified with the superficialities of the 'aesthetes' of the 'nineties. He didn't claim that art was 'above' morality. He is as much of a moralist as George Eliot, insisting on 'the perfect dependence of the "moral" sense of a work of art on the amount of felt life concerned in producing it' (see *Novelists on the Novel*, op. cit., pp. 99–100). When one says that James is the most refined of novelists, one isn't implying that he is less concerned than, say, Dickens with life and the moral discriminations it demands; but it does mean that the idea of 'refinement' (with its undertones of social sophistication and élitism) is pretty basic to the sensibility of which James's novels are an expression.

The point I'm suggesting is that the gap between the 'good' and the 'popular' (it was to be expressed later in the terms 'highbrow' and 'lowbrow')—one of the consequences of the development not just of commercial publishing but of the whole social, economic and political structure of Victorian England— involved a new role for the serious novelist which had consequences both social and aesthetic. The artist (like, indeed, intellectuals in general) tended to withdraw into a special area where he had a great deal of freedom to develop his own talents, interests and ideas, but not much direct contact with the mass of the people nor any part in the vital decisions taken by those who actually held power. It's one of the characteristics of the late Victorian and Edwardian intelligentsia that they tended to feel superior both to those who *did* have power in their society and those who *didn't*. (E. M. Forster's *Howards End* is a novel all about this phenomenon; so, earlier on, are George Eliot's *Felix Holt*, Henry James's *The Princess Casamassima* and George Meredith's *Beauchamp's Career*). The 'highbrow' writer of the end of the century was, at the same time, protecting himself from what he felt to be the corrupting influences of commercialism and the vulgarity of the masses. A typical example is Matthew Arnold, who in his *Culture and Anarchy* brilliantly evokes what seem to him to be the characteristics of the three divisions of Victorian society: aristocracy (Barbarians), middle class (Philistines) and Populace (who tear down the railings of Hyde Park). Since he is equally opposed to all three, the difficulties of achieving a satisfactory vantage-point, or point of view, from which to conduct his own operations as an intellectual are obvious. Arnold's answer is to define 'culture' in terms not of actual activity or relationships but in terms of ideal values ('sweetness and light'). George Eliot's and Henry James's positions are not very different from Arnold's. George Eliot is the more conscientiously 'responsible', James the more apt to see 'art' as self-justifying. George Eliot will often try to modify the sense of her 'superiority' by including herself in the strictures she feels bound to make about humanity in general ('Dear blunderers, I am one of you', *Theophrastus Such*). She is insistent on classifying herself among the 'struggling, erring human creatures' (see above). But such protests don't, I think, succeed in democratizing her attitudes in the more fundamental ways. Rather, they tend to create a sense of general human powerlessness in which the distinction of the artist is that he faces unpalatable human truths (such as 'as ye sow, so shall ye reap') more stoically than the mass of erring mortals. It's hard to arrive at any definition of the word 'popular' that would include *Middlemarch*, any more than *What Maisie Knew*, in a 'popular' tradition.

In this discussion I have been contrasting the artistic stance of George Eliot and Henry James with that of their predecessors, especially Dickens, and I've suggested that changing approaches to novel-writing are fairly closely connected with general social and cultural developments in Britain after the 1840s and especially with the increasing isolation of the intelligentsia and the growing gap between 'good' and 'popular' literature. I must make clear, though, that in making these points about the art of George Eliot and James I'm not implying any easy or automatic value-judgements. The value of *Mansfield Park* isn't automatically lessened by Jane Austen's personal fidelity to an essentially aristocratic scale of values; nor is the value of *Middlemarch* or *Maisie* necessarily undermined by an insistence that there was, after Dickens, a general tendency to turn away from the conception of a unifying popular culture.

How does Hardy fit into this general picture? Would you feel that, as with George Eliot and Henry James, he tends to move away from a 'popular' tradition?

Discussion

I can't predict your answer to that question. You may have argued that Hardy's novels (taking *Tess* as an example) weren't designed for a 'mass' audience, that his readership, though considerable, was basically middle-class, and that his idiom, unlike Dickens's, isn't close to that of the popular entertainer. All this is true. And the fact that he was prepared to mutilate his novels in the cause of serial publication (see Units 17–18) is evidence of his ambiguous attitude to the 'popular' market.

Or you may have argued that Hardy's subject-matter is much more 'plebeian' or 'lower-class' than George Eliot's or James's, that he writes with close sympathy of the struggles and dilemmas of humble but aspiring people, and that there is no suggestion of superiority in his attitudes. *Tess* certainly has one of the qualities one associates with 'popular' rather than 'highbrow' fiction—a very strong sense of human indignation. Again, Hardy, though a well-educated man who kept abreast of the intellectual development of the day, isn't a sophisticated writer: his observations about intellectual matters have, rather, the tone of the self-educated man. He may lack in *Tess* the confident, 'popular' touch which characterizes Dickens's description of Pip's adventures; but there can't be any doubt about his 'point of view' as far as Tess's aspirations are concerned. Tess belongs, socially, to the 'common people'; but Hardy would never give the word 'common' the flavour George Eliot gives it.

In other words, it all depends how you use the word 'popular'.

If you use the word as a contrast to 'élitist' or 'high-brow'; if you associate it with a closeness to the aspirations and sensibility of those whom Dickens described as 'The People governed' as opposed to 'the people governing',[1]

[1]'My faith in the people governing, is, on the whole, infinitesimal; my faith in The People governed, is, on the whole, illimitable'—Dickens at the Birmingham and Midland Institute, 27th September 1869. NB In subsequent correspondence he insisted on capital letters for his use of The People who are governed.

then it seems right to associate Hardy with a popular tradition and to stress his affinities with Dickens rather than George Eliot.

3 Dickens, George Eliot and 'the growing good of the world'

(By Angus Calder)

There are other ways of looking at Dickens and George Eliot. I want to consider how both writers implicitly viewed what I would call a typical Victorian notion—'the growing good of the world', or the idea of inevitable progress in human affairs.

The idea of 'rising in the world', which was dear to many when Dickens and George Eliot were writing, and very much in tune with the liberal individualism and the 'free enterprise' spirit of many Victorians, is set in a savagely ironical light in *Great Expectations*. Magwitch, for all his hard work in Australia, cannot 'rise' to social acceptability. Pip 'rises' to idleness and dissipation, and the jeers of Trabb's boy are fairly aimed at his pretensions. Yet the implications of all this may be blurred (I suggested this in effect in Unit 11) by the stereotyped sentimentalization of Joe. The book's early readers didn't find it subversively radical and Dickens, as we know, had apparently gone out of his way to 'let them down lightly' when he revised the end of the novel. I'd like you now to re-read the last chapter of *Great Expectations*, noting your answers to these questions:

1 What do you think Dickens is up to in introducing a replica Pip, son of Joe and Biddy? (Remember—Joe is *not* a blood relation of Philip Pirrip himself!)

2 Would you defend the 'revised' ending of the novel which follows Pip's conversation with Biddy, and if so, on what grounds?

Discussion

My answers:

1 I *could* use this to support the point that Dickens is sentimental. After all we have 'seen' in the novel, to think of another Pip growing up in the dreary marshlands, by the same old forge, should surely *not* appeal to us? There's old Joe, same as ever, 'though a little grey', contented in his 'station' in life: standing still. There's Biddy, once a lively, self-educative girl, reduced to the role of contented housewife ('good matronly hand') in this boring place. But Pip, who escaped from the marshes—and who clearly will never *live* there again—approves of the whole domestic scene. Even in the days before heredity was fully understood, Dickens must have realized that a replica Pip is only possible, from this union, if we assume Joe or Biddy to have been a by-blow of some randy Pirrip! Yet there he is, fenced in by Joe's same old leg. This is sentimental, surely? And preposterous?

2 Yes, but by the same 'common sense' standard, so is the name, Philip Pirrip, of our narrator hero. Giving Pip such a name, Dickens tipped us off on his first page that his novel couldn't be read as 'literally true to everyday life', as a 'slice of life'. (If you have any doubts about what I mean here, please re-read what Graham Martin says in Section 3 of Unit 7.) And I would defend the revised ending on this basis. It clinches the quasi-poetic character of the whole book.

You will remember that Dickens makes an important allusion to Milton's *Paradise Lost*. Could you now re-read what your Study Guide to the novel, Unit 6, pp. 13–14, has to say about the last few paragraphs of the 'first stage'? What is their relation to the novel's ending?

Discussion

Well, they have both a structural and a 'poetic' relationship. Obviously, the end of the 'first stage' and the end of the 'third stage' have at least the same kind of relationship to each other as two columns in a row of four under one pediment. But there's also a dynamic, 'poetic' link. Whereas at the opening of the book and at the end of the 'second stage' the dominant element in the weather is *wind*, the *mists* of page 186 return (as it were) on page 491 and this recurrence reinforces the Miltonic echo. Adam and Eve leave the Garden of Eden of Milton's epic:

> The World was all before them, where to choose
> Thir place of rest, and Providence thir guide:
> They hand in hand with wandring steps and slow,
> Through *Eden* took thir solitary way.

In the last paragraph of *Great Expectations*, Pip and Estella, hand in hand, leave—what?

A ruined garden! The revised ending is richly suggestive in its imagery. The setting has its innate pathos, enhanced by the mists and the moon, both linked explicitly with earlier passages in the novel. The link back to page 186 enforces a parallel—Pip leaving the forge was *like* Pip and Estella leaving the ruins of Satis House, which is *like* Adam and Eve leaving Eden although, of course, not exactly the *same*. Yet Pip's life before leaving the forge was as miserable as Estella's at Satis House. Each environment was by implication 'like Eden', the sphere of innocence, yet neither was paradisal in any obvious way. What the revised ending implies, for me, is that Pip and Estella leave with the world 'all before them' (that 'broad expanse of tranquil light'). They are 'sadder but wiser'. Like Adam and Eve, they put both innocence and their 'fall' behind them. But what has been lost, the scope of innocence, will still be desired.

So I can even justify the 'replica' Pip: reading the novel as if it were like a poem with meanings packed into a rich pattern of imagery. To adopt terms from William Blake, the later Pip represents lost 'innocence', Pip and Estella the world of 'experience'.

Apparently, Pip 'progresses'. He 'rises in the world' . . . But it turns out that the sphere of his 'innocence' has values which haunt him after adult 'experience', though escape from the world of his childhood is fundamental to all he is. Human life, for Dickens, is very complicated. It does not, simply, 'progress'. The melancholy-yet-affirmative tone of the revised ending of *Great Expectations* cuts right across simplistic ideas of 'progress'.

'Progress' is one of the key 'Victorian' notions. People tended to assume that man had progressed quite steadily, from the middle ages onwards at least, and that progress in science, in technology, and in the economy were being matched by equal progress in social institutions and in morality. The good of the world was growing, and would not stop growing. And 'England' (Victorians, even north of the Border, used this term for the whole island) was leading the world in its progress. It was the freest country in the world, with the best Constitution, the biggest Empire, the most advanced industries—and the best Christian morality.

You'll remember Samuel Smiles from Unit 11. In *Self-Help* (1859) Smiles wrote:

> Such as England is, she has been made by the thinking and working of many generations; the action of even the least significant person having contributed towards the production of the general result. Laborious and patient men of all ranks—cultivators of the soil and explorers of the mines—inventors and discoverers—tradesmen, mechanics, and labourers—poets, thinkers and politicians—all have worked together, one generation carrying forward the labours of another . . . This succession of noble workers—the artisans of civilization—has created order out of chaos, in industry, science, and art . . .

> Life . . . is a 'soldier's battle', the greatest workers in all times having been men in the ranks. Many are the lives of men unwritten, which have nevertheless as powerfully influenced civilization and progress as the more fortunate Great whose names are recorded in biography. Even the humblest person, who sets before his fellows an example of industry, sobriety and upright honesty of purpose in life, has a present as well as a future influence upon the well-being of his country; for his life and character pass unconsciously into the lives of others, and propagate good example for all time to come.

When, some years ago, I was first taking notes from *Self-Help*, I wrote beneath the quotation, on the card I've just copied that from, 'cf. George Eliot'. Could you now look at the last page of *Middlemarch*? Do you agree with me that George Eliot implies a similar view to Smiles's? (I'm *not* suggesting that George Eliot was 'influenced' by Smiles. As Cicely Havely implied in her discussion of Burke in relation to Jane Austen (Unit 2, pp. 22–24), thinkers and artists may express independently common preoccupations and notions of their age.) If not, what sentences of hers would you use to contradict me?

Discussion

Well, I think that her view *is* similar to Smiles's but that she implicitly contradicts herself—and she does so because she's far subtler than Smiles. My thoughts:

(a) 'The growing good of the world' implies progress, and as a phrase in itself seems smug.

(b) The tone of the last two paragraphs is very much that of a Victorian moralist— she's on the lecture platform with her specs on, D. H. Lawrence might have said.

(c) Like Smiles, she extols the virtue of 'hidden lives', by implication those of poor as well as of prosperous people: there's a democratic slant to her moralizing.

(d) Like Smiles, only more explicitly, she seems to think that there is no scope for grand gestures in existing society with its 'growing good', and in both cases I'd argue that this involves consciously or unconsciously minimizing the existence of social conflict. There *was* scope for heroism, I'd argue—in the creation of a working-class movement, in the struggle for women's rights, and so on. But George Eliot either doesn't see that, or doesn't want us to see that she sees it.

So far, I'm making out George Eliot to be a pretty conventional representative of a liberal Victorian trust in progress combined with faith in the essential stability of the social order. But the last word of all in *Middlemarch* is 'tombs'. And these two final paragraphs are shot through with sadness. Dorothea did struggle amid the conditions of an *'imperfect'* social state. George Eliot seems to regret that 'ardent deeds' are no longer appropriate, and yet also to recognize that our actions in our imperfect society are creating conditions against which *future* Dorotheas will rise up in struggle, which may be 'sadder' in outcome than hers.

When George Eliot published this novel, in the 1870s, complacency about 'English' society and its 'progress' were due to wane. Dickens had attacked it, with astonishing savagery, in his last completed novel *Our Mutual Friend* (1865). Two striking novelists of the younger generation, George Meredith and Thomas Hardy, were notably sceptical about such social pieties as, for instance, the idea that women's place was in the home. Writing as we do about a 'Victorian period' from 1837 to 1901, we are liable to confuse ourselves. Victoria's reign really covered several 'periods'. Till 1848 her realm was in social turmoil. From then till the mid-1860s unprecedented prosperity produced what has been called an 'Age of Equipoise'. Thereafter, equipoise was shattered.

Have a look at your Chronological Wall-Chart. British complacency was challenged by the rise of other industrial powers—the USA, recently-united Germany. The new technology showed its horrific side in the American Civil War and the Franco-Prussian war—mechanized wars and ones involving conscription. The challenge of communists and socialists to the bourgeois order was crystallized in the formation by Marx and others of the First International in London (1864). 1871 saw the brief life of the revolutionary Paris Commune. Of this, the historian Eric Hobsbawm writes:

> If it did not threaten the bourgeois order seriously, it frightened the wits out of it by its mere existence. Its life and death were surrounded by panic and hysteria, especially in the international press, which accused it of instituting communism, expropriating the rich and sharing their wives, terror, wholesale massacre, chaos, anarchy and whatever else haunted the nightmares of the respectable classes—all, needless to say, deliberately plotted by the International. (*The Age of Capital, 1848–1875*, page 167)

Meanwhile the second Reform Act of 1867 had extended the vote in Britain to working-class men. Feminist ideas were being expressed, not only in relation to suffrage, but in practical efforts to gain higher education for women. And prolonged agricultural depression set in, creating conditions for Thomas Hardy's apparent 'pessimism'.

Now the idea of 'progress' was clearly problematical in such circumstances. The Smilesian formulas depend on 'equipoise'. So long as society can plausibly be seen as progressing in 'good' directions, it can automatically claim the loyalty of everyone, rich and poor alike, thought of as partners in a common noble effort. If the idea of progress becomes dubious, then all social institutions likewise become suspect. And George Eliot did have her own suspicions. The smugness suggested to me by the conclusion to *Middlemarch* certainly isn't there, for example, in *Daniel Deronda* (1876), in which such matters as the concept of the 'gentleman', the role of women in society, and the general rightness of conventional English views, are subjected to quite fierce discussion. So, you might ask, why didn't the Course Team set *Daniel Deronda*, a brave book, rather than *Middlemarch*, a tamer one?

I think the decision suggested itself because *Middlemarch* is a superbly constructed 'work of art', while *Daniel Deronda* is much more 'uneven', much less 'satisfactory'. I am, however, disturbed—as perhaps you will be—by what I have just said. It seems to imply that the 'highest' achievements in English fiction may be based on a cheat. I want to believe that form and content are inseparable in a well-achieved work of art—how can unsatisfactory 'content' march with superb 'form'? Yet, despite its limitations, *Middlemarch* is stimulating, powerful and haunting, and I can't separate its power from its impressive technique. Rather than work right through these complicated questions, I want to leave you with some ideas to think about.

1   Is it the case that a certain kind of 'formal' achievement in fiction (as in other arts?) may depend on the novelist's feeling able, because the times are fairly comfortable, to smooth the rough edges off life and so produce harmony and neatness? Think how important the 'happy-ending-with-marriage' is as a formal device in British fiction, even in *Wuthering Heights*. What does it imply? That British readers want from fiction nothing but 'romantic' satisfaction and so go along with a convention which novelists like because it solves the problem of how to structure a tale? (Whereas French readers seem to be more 'cynical', and Russian readers accept *un*happy endings as the norm?) I think this is indeed part of the answer: British readers in general probably were more 'earnest' than readers in France, though less critical of social conventions than were many Russian readers. But *why* are British readers prepared to swallow the utterly un-'realistic' convention that a marriage contracted by young people can be taken as solving their problems for life? (I'm not exaggerating: think, if you've read it, of the end of *Tom Jones*. Ask yourself what could *possibly* disturb the tomb-like calm of the life together of Fanny and Edmund, as Jane Austen evokes it.)

Well, this convention surely couldn't be propagated by good writers addressing earnest readers within a 'realistic' mode of fiction if reality contradicted it too obviously. In Britain, I suggest, reality didn't. Despite periods of serious social disturbance, British society was never revolutionized, as French society repeatedly was, and as thinking Russians always expected their own society to be. Someone married in the 1830s to a politician might have gone through some anxious moments in the days of Chartism and mass unemployment— but not armed struggle, sudden reversal of fortune, rents in the whole social fabric of which marriage was part. A young man going East as a businessman at about the same time might have had deep worries connected with the Opium Wars with China and the Mutiny in India—but the Empire continued to thrive and expand, and Britain remained a safe country to come back to.

In short, Dorothea would not have been called upon to test her heroism on either side of a set of barricades, and Pip could have worked pretty steadily on, seeing a regular return for his efforts. A Frenchman, on the other hand, writing in 1788 as if happy marriage or hard work would solve a person's problems, or any European doing so in 1913, would have looked foolish to suggest any such thing.

2   Arising from this, might you agree with me that the formal control of *Great Expectations* and *Middlemarch*, that quality of authority which the narrators possess, can, and should, be related to the fact that each novel is set about forty years before? As highly intelligent people full of social concern, both novelists must have been uneasily aware that British society, as they wrote, was more fragile than they, or their readers, liked to think. But without obvious dishonesty they could *order* events dated back to a time since when no *major* upheaval would have diverted their characters' lives. The past was 'tame'. In *Our Mutual Friend*, in *Daniel Deronda*, the 'wild' present was too rough and disturbing to be fully ordered.

3   I am suggesting that *Middlemarch* embodies 'conventional' Victorian attitudes which are built even into its narrative form. Is this as damning as it

sounds? One type of critic, alleging what I've alleged, would seem to imply that 'novels are just ideology wrapped up in stories. Studying these middle-class fables is useful because it shows us how Victorian ideology worked and can help us to expose it.' But I myself don't want to imply any such thing. I believe that 'ideology' is a much more complicated business than many people assume, because the reality which it springs from, and which it influences in its turn, is so complex.

Suppose we agreed that a 'typical' Victorian ideology involved extolling individual effort and hard work, pretending that all prosperity stemmed from them, keeping women 'in their place' by invoking the sacredness of marriage, adopting racialist views to explain and condone the subjugation of coloured peoples in the interests of Britain's profits, and extolling Britain's progress . . . Suppose we further agreed that the following thinkers were amongst the most influential in Victorian England, so must be regarded as in some way 'typical': Carlyle, Ruskin, Mill . . . Well, what nonsense we would have fallen into! Three thinkers more different, in style, direction, temperament, one could hardly imagine. Putting it crudely: Carlyle was a racialist and a believer in 'aristocratic' rule; Ruskin was an imperialist; Mill was the prime exponent of liberal individualism. But Carlyle was not a liberal individualist; and Mill was not a racialist, and argued for the equality of women. Smiles, far inferior as a thinker and as a stylist to all the three I've named, hardly fits the 'typical Victorian' label better than they do. As I pointed out in Unit 11, he was explicitly critical of Victorian middle-class values. And in his confused way he did believe that ordinary people, including manual workers, had as much right to respect as the rich. Victorian society (like our own) was ridden by contradictions. Christian faith, in an age of advancing science and successful materialism, caused at least as many problems for believers as it solved. Liberal individualism and the cult of 'free trade' went very uneasily indeed with the maintenance and expansion of a vast overseas empire. Dickens and George Eliot didn't operate in a society where a monolithic ruling class had successfully imposed a single coherent set of ideas on everyone. Conventions could often be seen for precisely what they were, conventions. Argument over moral and social issues was earnest and persistent. Hypocrisy in one's opponents would be swiftly and fiercely exposed. I think that, despite elements of smugness and delusion, *Great Expectations* and *Middlemarch* remain 'alive' for us partly because their authors are responding vividly to an atmosphere of debate. Some questions raised in that debate have still not been settled. And their *stories*, shaped in relation to nineteenth-century ideas though they are, have an intrinsic strength. We don't discard Homer because we have ceased to believe in Zeus, or Bunyan because we're no longer (most of us) Bible Christians. We reinterpret, almost re*write*, the great stories so that they make sense in our own time. When this can't be done any longer, the books will 'die', except for scholars.

4   A feminist point of view

(By Joan Bellamy)

The contemporary feminist movement, which has expanded so rapidly since the late 1960s, has carried forward traditional demands for equal rights for women and has also initiated important research into many areas of intellectual life, including the development of feminist literary criticism. This note offers, first, a description of some of the issues that are now being discussed by feminist critics and, secondly, comments on some questions to do with the women characters in a few of the novels in the course.

Today our ideas about the place of women in society and about family and sexual relationships are changing and have become very different from the views that were predominant in the nineteenth century. Consequently, we look at the novels of that time in new ways, ways that are affected by our changing consciousness. As Angus Calder has just said, 'we reinterpret, almost *rewrite*, the great stories so that they make sense in our own time'. Feminist criticism's basic point of departure is that women have for centuries occupied a socially subordinate and underprivileged position but that they are now calling that position into question. The evaluations and 'rewritings' of feminist criticism are an attempt to reveal how works of literature operate either in upholding or challenging women's subordination.

Just as feminism in general challenges long-accepted attitudes to women, so feminist criticism disturbs more familiar critical approaches to literature; and we should not be surprised if it is met, sometimes with incomprehension, sometimes with angry responses—the opposing sides not necessarily being ranged according to sex. There is no single unified school of feminist criticism, and there is lively debate amongst feminists themselves, but most would agree that the way literature depicts women reveals something important about the society which produces and reads it, something too about the influence of literature on the way we think, feel and behave.

Women in an alien world

A frequently debated issue in the feminist movement is why there are relatively few women creative artists. As early as 1929 Virginia Woolf, in *A Room of One's Own*, was asking if women writers face special difficulties: are there conventional 'male-dominated' ways of looking at literature which fail to give full credit to the intrinsic value of women's specific experiences and the writing that embodies them? Do women writers find it difficult to write good novels, and has their work been distorted, because of pressures to meet the requirements of alien values imposed from outside feminine sensibility? Referring particularly to nineteenth-century writers, she says:

> One has only to skim those old forgotten novels and listen to the tone of voice in which they are written to divine that the writer was meeting criticism; she was saying this by way of aggression, or that by way of conciliation. She was admitting that she was 'only a woman', or protesting that she was 'as good as a man'. She met that criticism as her temperament dictated, with docility and diffidence, or with anger and emphasis. It does not matter which it was; she was thinking of something other than the thing itself. Down comes her book upon our heads. There was a flaw in the centre of it. And I thought of all the women's novels that lie scattered, like small pock-marked apples in an orchard, about the second-hand books shops of London. It was the flaw in the centre that had rotted them. She had altered her values in deference to the opinion of others.
>
> But how impossible it must have been for them not to budge either to the right or to the left. What genius, what integrity it must have required in face of all that criticism, in the midst of that purely patriarchal society, to hold fast to the thing as they saw it without shrinking. Only Jane Austen did it and Emily Brontë. It is another feather, perhaps the finest, in their caps. They wrote as women write, not as men write. (*A Room of One's Own*, page 71)

Woolf is expressing here the 'double-bind' problem for women aspiring to new forms of freedom and expression: the difficulty of working within a male-dominated system of values while being alienated from it; the need both to declare one's independence from that male world and yet at the same time to participate in it, even conquer it. Mary Jacobus, in the part of her essay 'The difference of view' reprinted in Units 12–14 (pp. 64ff.), shows how Woolf tends to see the aspiring woman writer in terms of suffering, burdens, and martyrdom (this is how Woolf sees George Eliot and perhaps herself) and how this appears to be the price the woman writer pays for seeking to invade male-dominated culture. By contrast, Jacobus suggests, modern feminists stress the joys of aspiring to self-realization and of achieving it.

Simply to mention these two contrasted positions, martyrdom to the male world and joyous female autonomy, is to demonstrate the complexity of feminist debate. There are many other difficult and important problems that feminist critics are also trying to face: aesthetic questions; the relationship between women's oppression and class oppression; the significance of specific features of different national histories and cultures; the question, indeed, whether there *is* a specific women's way of looking at life. Mary Jacobus touches, too, on the problem of language. Many feminists are now discussing the way in which language is biased towards male experience and needs and the extent to which this reinforces the male domination from which feminists are seeking to free themselves. Most of us know the frustration of seeing 'he' used as the generic pronoun, when women are meant also: the reader, the student, the critic, the voter, is always 'he'. When a feminist critic, like Ellen Moers in *Literary Women*, consistently uses 'she' instead, or coins the word 'heroinism', we are jolted very directly into a new perception of the limitations of our language and the way we use it.

Feminist criticism and the nineteenth-century novel

The literature of the nineteenth century has attracted a great deal of attention from feminist critics. One reason is that considerable numbers of women in the nineteenth century seized the opportunity, offered by the expanding publishing industry, of earning a living by writing instead of through badly paid work as governesses and teachers. Even for those who did not need to earn a living, writing offered important opportunities for self-expression and intellectual activity at a time when higher education and most of the professions were closed to women. Feminist literary historians are interested in the achievements, preoccupations and concerns of these writers, many of whom are now being rediscovered. They want to find out why their work came to be neglected (often after considerable success), how they expressed their perception of women's experiences, whether they learned from one another, and whether they were influenced by the new women's movement of their time. The nineteenth-century novel, with its familiar themes of women's rebellion and aspirations for an independent, active and responsible life, seems to have close links with the growth of women's demands for reforms, suffrage, and other kinds of equality (though it would be wrong to treat the novels as if they were feminist tracts).

The nineteenth-century novel attracts feminist critics too because of its commitment to realism and its frequently combined concern with moral responsibility and family relationships, love and marriage. It offers a particularly rich field of investigation into the connections between literature, women's position in society, and views about women's social and moral function. This has stimulated a particularly active line of feminist criticism, concerned with the kinds of women *characters* created by the nineteenth-century novelists, the pictures of women these writers give in the worlds they create for us, the destinies they offer for their heroines, the kinds of language, imagery, plot and narrative comment they employ, and the writers' and readers' assumptions, explicit and implicit, that are thereby revealed. This, then, brings us to our second concern in this note: the women characters in some of the novels of the course.

Jane Austen takes us into the life of the country gentry, living quietly and privately: the men engaged in running their estates and administering local and, occasionally, national politics; younger brothers in the army, navy or established church. It is a seemingly stable and quiet world in which it is assumed that the women lead calm, protected lives in the shelter of their prosperous and elegant homes, in families ruled by wise and benevolent, if firm, patriarchs. This is the world Austen knew intimately, and in *Mansfield Park* she moves beneath these surface assumptions to set before us a complex picture of a world strained by the tensions between objective needs and subjective inclinations, between society and individual. Her young women go through acute moral crises in a society in which it is imperative for them to marry—in which marriage is an alliance between class-conscious families concerned to promote their wealth and social consequence. How is an honourable young woman to live a moral life, marry for love, and yet take account of the realities of the world in which she lives, where money and position, duty, and the demands of social life also have their rightful claims? Fanny's heroism consists in cherishing her love for Edmund without attempting to manipulate him in order to 'catch him' for herself, and in rejecting Crawford even though her refusal violates her deep sense of obligation and duty to both Edmund and Sir Thomas.

The pressures on Fanny to marry Crawford are rather different from those which push Maria Bertram into recklessly contracting a loveless marriage. Humiliated by Crawford's manipulation and rejection of her feelings, Maria seeks the social security and status that only a wealthy marriage can bring a woman in her position; and she is seeking to escape from strong patriarchal control. For her, the consequences of breaking the conventions are banishment for ever from society and her family; on the other hand Henry Crawford will, one feels, be taken back into fashionable society, once more the eligible bachelor.

We sense in the novel that the traditional world of the gentry, with its country estates, its central position in political life, its remoteness from the world of commerce and industry, is under threat. Angus Calder has written about the way that Samuel Smiles's work reflected the growth of opportunities in the nineteenth century for men who wanted to get on in the world of expanding industrial capitalism. For middle-class women, opportunities were becoming relatively narrower. With the increase in middle-class prosperity and growing aspirations to gentility, women were increasingly excluded from direct participation in the economic life of the family: they were cut off from the new professions and were confined to the home and family life, now seen only as wives and mothers, comforters, female dependants, and domestic auxiliaries. Their 'compensation' for social isolation was to exercise a pure and beneficent moral influence, preferably through self-sacrifice. This was not an exclusively male conspiracy against women's freedom—it was joined and supported by considerable numbers of women who actively justified it:

> Can it be a subject of regret that she is not called upon, so much as man, to calculate, to compete, to struggle, but rather to occupy a sphere in which the elements of discord cannot, with propriety, be admitted—in which beauty and order are expected to denote her presence, and where the exercise of benevolence is the duty she is most frequently called upon

to perform? (Sarah Stickney Ellis, *The Daughters of England*, 1850; quoted in C. Bauer and L. Ritt (eds.), *Free and Ennobled*, pp. 13–14)

In *Great Expectations*, Wemmick's toytown house in Walworth and his 'After I have crossed this bridge, I hoist it up—so—and cut off the communication' (page 229) perfectly expresses the image of the nineteenth-century middle-class home as a secret private place of relaxation insulated from the pressures of the world outside. It is a refuge for the male breadwinner, battling for success in the corrupt world outside. But for many of the women enclosed within it, it is a veritable prison. Dickens here offers us a view of middle-class suburban domesticity both comic and cosy, but domestic life occupies his attention only briefly, and mainly as a counterpoint to the realities of the male world outside. Nevertheless, although domestic life is not Dickens's main concern in *Great Expectations*, since he is tracing the moral growth of a hero, the treatment of the women characters in the novel is still of interest, even if only one aspect of a rich and complex novel.

The preface to your edition recalls that Tolstoy believed that Dickens loved his characters and that this was one of the secrets of his popularity. One can't, of course, doubt Dickens's popularity, but I am not so sure about his love for all his characters. Certainly, there seem to be contradictions between Dickens's imaginative energy and critical vision on the one hand, and, on the other, the inadequate realization of so many of his women characters. I am made particularly uneasy by his treatment in this novel of the characters one may term the 'recalcitrant women', like Miss Havisham, Estella, Mrs Joe, and Estella's mother. For Pip, there is redemption through his growing love and protection of Magwitch, and his good deed on behalf of Herbert; for Miss Havisham, redemption is only through death by fire, and for Estella (with a 'saddened softened light of the once proud eyes', and now capable of loving) through her experience of suffering 'stronger than all other teaching'. She hints at Drummond's depriving her of wealth; with our vision of his brutality to the horse, are we to assume he beat Estella too? Are there not also sadistic elements in the scene where Jaggers—whose fundamental impulse, beneath his bullying and his manipulation of the law, is compassionate—nevertheless forces Estella's mother to show the strength of her wrists?

> Her entrapped hand was on the table, but she had already put her other hand behind her waist. 'Master,' she said, in a low voice, with her eyes attentively and entreatingly fixed upon him. 'Don't.'
>
> '*I*'ll show you a wrist,' repeated Mr Jaggers, with an immovable determination to show it. 'Molly, let them see your wrist.'
>
> 'Master,' she again murmured. 'Please!'
>
> 'Molly,' said Mr Jaggers, not looking at her, but obstinately looking at the opposite side of the room, 'let them see *both* your wrists. Show them. Come!' (Penguin ed., page 236)

Jaggers later tells Pip that the woman went to him 'to be sheltered', but we are offered a vision of a wild beast scarcely tamed: '. . . he kept down the old wild violent nature whenever he saw an inkling of its breaking out, by asserting his power over her in the old way' (page 425). Estella's mother seems a kind of Mrs Rochester of the criminal classes, the violent bestial madwoman threatening violent death to men and controlled only by force and threats.

Jaggers represents a certain sort of power, and in the nineteenth-century novel women are excluded from power, whether over their own fates or anyone else's. Power is for men and it seems in the nature of things that they should hold it. Miss Havisham misuses hers and dies. Joe abdicates power over Mrs Joe because of his father's brutality to his mother, but Mrs Joe has nevertheless to be 'tamed', brutally struck down by Orlick (so like Drummle) with the iron that shackled 'my convict'. She has been struck from behind, not even during a quarrel, and when she finally succeeds in getting Orlick brought into the house 'there was an air of humble propitiation in all she did, such as I have seen pervade the bearing of a child towards a hard master' (page 151). The women are reduced to a childlike level and are mastered by male force, as Estella's mother is by Jaggers: 'master' is a key word in both these descriptions.

You may recall here the phrase George Eliot uses as Lydgate recognizes the danger to his marriage in Rosamond's passive resistance: 'It would assuredly have been a vain boast in him to say that he was her master' (*Middlemarch*, Penguin ed., page 718). *Middlemarch*, the most ambitious of the English novels in our course, creates a rich interplay of character and personal relations within a wider social life; and Middlemarch society relegates women to a subordinate and dependent place in marriage and nourishes general illusions about their nature which threaten personal happiness. Casaubon thinks Dorothea will be 'as a little moon that would cause hardly a perturbation', while Lydgate imagines marriage as a 'paradise with sweet laughs for bird notes and blue eyes for a heaven'. Rosamund, perfectly trained for the conventional marriage-market, turns out to be a 'pot of basil feeding on men's brains', undermining and destroying Lydgate's happiness and professional hopes. Dorothea's marriage to Casaubon turns out to be sterile and blighted.

To what extent can we regard George Eliot as a feminist writer? Barbara Hardy, in *The Novels of George Eliot*, suggests that Eliot's feminism is brought under strict control by her creation of the two parallel tragedies, Lydgate's and Dorothea's. I see the parallel stories as illustrating interacting aspects of the effects of a marriage system which has as its primary victims women such as Dorothea, but which can also undermine and destroy the dominant male—even (and especially perhaps) one as attractive and admirable as Lydgate. For Lydgate there are two tragedies, the failure of his career and of his marriage. Dorothea's situation is summarized in the epigraph heading the first chapter:

> Since I can do no good because a woman,
> Reach constantly at something that is near it.

Her obvious tragedy is the disastrous marriage to Casaubon, which she overcomes by sheer force of moral character and from which she is rescued by the accident of her husband's death. But can we with any confidence take her second marriage as a 'happy' ending? Has she a second tragedy too?

Barbara Hardy shows how the conclusion of the first, serialized edition of *Middlemarch* blamed society for Dorothea's mistake:

> Among the many remarks passed on her mistake, it was never said in the neighbourhood of Middlemarch that such mistakes could not have happened if the society into which she was born had not smiled on propositions of marriage from a sickly man to a girl less than half his own age . . . on modes of education which make a woman's knowledge another name for motley ignorance . . . on rules of conduct which are in flat contradiction with its own loudly asserted beliefs. (Quoted in *The Novels of George Eliot*, page 52)

Compare this with the conclusion in your edition (page 896). The earlier certainty is reduced by phrases like 'not ideally beautiful', 'imperfect social state', 'error', 'illusion'. Eliot perhaps noticed, too, her own inconsistency.

Middlemarch 'society' had *not* smiled on Casaubon's 'propositions of marriage' to Dorothea, quite the contrary. Dorothea's determination to accept Casaubon is evidence of her immature arrogance and of the illusions nurtured by her ignorance. But Eliot goes beyond eliminating the inconsistency. She cuts out references to women being deprived of the kind of education which would equip them to live more happily, though that theme pervades the whole book. Mary and Mrs Garth exemplify the educated woman: they are both shrewd, knowledgeable and resourceful, and their education is offered as a partial explanation of their control and moral influence, though even they engage in continuous (though loving) subterfuges to maintain the fiction of their husbands' superiority.

The vague, ambivalent conclusion is already foreshadowed in the Prelude, with its uneasy, tentative language. While asserting women's individuality and deploring the view that they are by nature unachieving, Eliot implies that frustration and unhappiness is not their general lot. She concludes that it is only 'Here and there' that a St Theresa is born, and *Middlemarch* has only one Dorothea, standing out from the rest who live more or less contentedly in their assigned role.

By placing the events of the novel in the period of the Reform Act, 1829–31, George Eliot excludes from her novel the sort of solutions for Dorothea which Florence Nightingale in life had pioneered in 1857, and which Turgenev in *On the Eve* seems to be reflecting in Elena's decision to join the Sisters of Mercy in the Balkans. If Eliot had set her novel later, Dorothea might, at a less heroic level perhaps, have been able to look for guidance, knowledge and fulfilment not at Lowick Manor but at Bedford College for Women, founded in 1853.

It's difficult to know how far *Middlemarch* accurately reflects George Eliot's own attitude to feminism and the women's movement. In its picture of a rich and complex social life, for which she drew on her own memories, the novel cannot be reduced to being only about 'the woman problem'. Nevertheless, there is a sense in which its opening propositions about women's social place promise more than they eventually yield, and the sense of fatalistically making the best of a bad situation lingers over the conclusion. In 1866, three years before she began work on *Middlemarch*, George Eliot had been asked to add her name to the very important petition for women's suffrage signed by a large number of distinguished women. Florence Nightingale declined to sign it, because she thought women had more important goals to reach than the winning of the vote, but George Eliot refused because she thought that women's harder lot ought to be 'the basis for a sublimer resignation in women and a more regenerating tenderness in men' (quoted in Gordon S. Haight, *George Eliot: a Biography*, page 396). This is an attitude which permeates *Middlemarch*.

The double standard, constraining women's sexuality while permitting men a greater sexual freedom, is seen to exist in *Mansfield Park*, *Great Expectations* and in *Middlemarch* but is only tentatively hinted at. *Anna Karenina*, on the other hand, opens brilliantly with the particular unhappiness of the Oblonsky family as Dolly contemplates the horror of Stepan's promiscuity. Tolstoy's brilliant control of this rich, epic-scale novel is immediately at work as we see Anna patching up the marriage. Fudging moral issues, she works on Dolly to make it up with Stepan, conspiring in a system of values in which women are less in control of their lives than men, who are permitted to indulge their sexual desires freely, commit adultery and wear out their wives through frequent pregnancies. It is a system of double values that will inexorably destroy Anna herself. Tolstoy intended originally to depict Anna as a seductress appropriately punished. His powerful imaginative insight created instead a heroine who engages our sympathies. Could he have allowed Anna to survive?

The constraints of the 'realist' novel, as well as Tolstoy's own strong patriarchal and religious views, appear to reinforce each other to prevent any other possible outcome and Anna is consigned to destruction. Dolly in turn looks forward to continuous anguish and self-sacrifice to her children. The two women are clearly victims—though perhaps an even darker side of their tragedy is their acceptance of society's view of themselves as guilty or as inevitably born to self-sacrifice.

Tolstoy's treatment of sexual relations, and indeed that of all the Continental novelists studied in the course, contrasts sharply with the way Dickens or Eliot present them (if at all). George Eliot herself practised contraception (as Tolstoy has Anna do), but in *Middlemarch* sexual experience is scarcely touched on, let alone anything like contraception. The language and imagery expressing Dorothea's misery and bewilderment on her Rome honeymoon suggest the non-consummation of the marriage, for those able to detect it, but there is nothing by way of an explicit statement from the author. For writers like Dickens and Eliot the pressures were apparently too great to risk treating sexual matters in an open and mature way.

A factor which influenced them was the power of the market, dominated by publishers and the owners of the lending libraries. One such was Mr Mudie, who strictly controlled the purchase of the novels offered in his lending libraries. He saw his customers as middle-class, respectable and what we would regard as repressive and prudish. No novel likely to be read aloud in the mixed family circle was to feature language or incidents which could bring a blush to the cheeks of young ladies, whose ignorance of the facts of life was assumed to be absolute. Prevailing views of marriage, domesticity and women's place in the home also led readers to expect marriage for the heroine as the inevitable, appropriate happy ending—marriage, that is, to the hero. Dickens yielded to pressure and offered a second, happy, alternative ending for *Great Expectations*, and we still debate which of his conclusions more truly reflects the structure and tone of the novel as a whole.

How does a fairy-tale ending square with 'realism', with the 'slice of life', when life does not always offer us the conclusion of the happy marriage, and when marriage turns out to be not an ending but a beginning, and not always a happy one? Is George Eliot, for example, cheating in marrying Dorothea to Ladislaw? I think not; on the contrary, I think she recognizes the tension in the outcome she offers, which is set off against the really conventional cosy ending of the Mary Garth—Fred Vincy story. Eliot saw herself as a witness to truth. She tells us in *Adam Bede*:

> I aspire to give no more than a faithful account of men and things as they have mirrored themselves in my mind. The mirror is doubtless defective, the outlines will sometimes be disturbed, the reflection faint or confused: *but I feel as much bound to tell you as precisely as I can what that reflection is*, as if I were in the witness box narrating my experience on oath. (Penguin ed., page 221; my italics)

She recognized the complexity of detecting what the truth is as well as the difficulty of telling it. Given Dorothea's restricted opportunities, and the 'real' world of *Middlemarch* and the England of the 1830s, how could Eliot have provided the happy-ever-after formula? As we have seen, she can hardly give Dorothea a career in politics or send her off nursing in the Balkans: that would represent fantasy. But she can't, as an honest witness, pass off the fairy-tale marriage either. What she offers us, then, is a marriage for Dorothea which is a move *down* the social scale. Dorothea will possibly have to make do on a few hundred a year (and live in a street!) and exist on the periphery of

Ladislaw's active life in politics; he will be the modern politician paid by his constituency, she his helpmate. We are to console ourselves, if we need to, with an uncertain vision of a general stream of ever growing good to which we all, Dorothea included, may contribute.

Short of the finality of the tragic ending in death, the alternative to happy marriage ever after seems to be the open ending, which concedes implicitly that the 'slice of life' we have been offered is not really a detached autonomous piece, but merely a stage in the continuous business of living. Eliot herself, after *Middlemarch*, offers the open-ended *Daniel Deronda*, with Gwendolen not married to Daniel but left to work her way through to a life of purpose and meaning, though one doesn't see at all how she will do it. Turgenev offers us doubt and mystery, as Elena's fate is reported to us. She disappears 'married' to a great cause, and in a sense her physical survival is not all that important; what we have experienced is the potential of a heroine, in a world on the eve of change and liberation, who finds freedom in identifying with a cause outside herself.

In Zola's open ending, Étienne walks out of one area of conflict and struggle towards another. It is Maheude who remains, changed by her experiences and facing hard toil and class conflict. But that is matter for another discussion, which would take us into a consideration of literature about the proletarian world and the relationship between class and sexual oppression. Such a discussion would move beyond the confines of novels whose world is that of the upper and middle classes, into the modern world of industrialization and a new working class. It is a world which feminist criticism, as it develops in range and depth, will also take into account, offering new insights from women's points of view.

Further reading

From the great range of critical books from a feminist viewpoint published in recent years, I have selected six which represent a variety of themes and approaches. Virginia Woolf's *A Room of One's Own* is, of course, something of a classic.

Calder, Jenni, *Women and Marriage in Victorian Fiction*, Thames and Hudson, 1976.

Jacobus, Mary (ed.), *Women Writing and Writing about Women*, Croom Helm, 1979.

Moers, Ellen, *Literary Women*, 1977; Women's Press, 1978.

Showalter, Elaine, *A Literature of Their Own: British Women Novelists from Brontë to Lessing*, Virago, 1978.

Spender, Dale, *Man Made Language*, Routledge and Kegan Paul, 1980.

Stubbs, Patricia, *Women and Fiction*, Harvester Press, 1979.

Woolf, Virginia, *A Room of One's Own*, 1929; Triad/Panther (Granada) ed., 1977.

5 Authorial discourse in the age of Darwin

(By John Goode)

I would like to begin by referring you once again to the opening of Chapter 15 of *Middlemarch*, which David Lodge discusses in his essay in the Course Reader (pp. 218 ff.). Before she embarks on the detailed anatomy of Lydgate's character, George Eliot pauses to talk to the reader about her own narrative method:

> A great historian, as he insisted on calling himself, who had the happiness to be dead a hundred and twenty years ago, and so to take his place among the colossi whose huge legs our living pettiness is observed to walk under, glories in his copious remarks and digressions as the least imitable part of his work, and especially in those initial chapters to the successive books of his history, where he seems to bring his arm-chair to the proscenium and chat with us in all the lusty ease of his fine English. But Fielding lived when the days were longer (for time, like money, is measured by our needs), when summer afternoons were spacious, and the clock ticked slowly in the winter evenings. We belated historians must not linger after his example; and if we did so, it is probable that our chat would be thin and eager, as if delivered from a camp-stool in a parrot-house. I at least have so much to do in unravelling certain human lots, and seeing how they were woven and interwoven, that all the light I can command must be concentrated on this particular web, and not dispersed over that tempting range of relevancies called the universe. (Penguin ed., page 170)

You might re-read this and the chapter which it introduces, thinking once more about the kind of writing it is, and the significance of what Eliot says about her own task as a novelist. Does this kind of passage *add* anything to the novel?

Discussion

I would suggest that it reminds us that there is an author *making* the novel, an author who seems to be totally in control of what is shown and the way in which it is to be interpreted. Many such passages occur in *Middlemarch*, forming a whole 'authorial discourse'. (By 'discourse' I mean a stretch of language larger than a sentence.) We may feel that this discourse limits the reality of the novel's world, because it presupposes an omniscient standpoint not available to us in life. It interferes with what I would call the 'mimetic validity' of the text, that is, the consistency of the illusion that the world presented may be 'real'.

George Eliot here contrasts her narrative method with that of Fielding—the most obvious case of a novelist who relies on authorial omniscience. The armchair and the proscenium pinpoint precisely the ways in which Fielding distances his narrative, making it conform to his moral and aesthetic presumptions: the story is mediated through a genial conversational voice, digressing freely and ensuring that we never forget that Fielding is the creator; and it is further 'stylized' by theatrical effects of confrontation, revelation and resolution. Here, in *Middlemarch*, we have a paradox—Eliot is using her authorial omniscience to *exclude* omniscience; she is generalizing about the impossibility of generalization.

41

One of the most persistent debates about narrative method, originating with Flaubert but remarkably dominant in Anglo-Saxon criticism from Henry James onwards, centres on this question of explicit authorial presence. True realism, one argument goes, depends on our sense that life is presented to us without rearrangement. Hence the author should eliminate himself as much as possible, and we should be given what we are given in life, immediate experience. In Hardy's phrase, the novel should be as much as possible 'a series of seemings'. This guarantees its authenticity. It is the attempt to achieve formal objectivity that motivates the late experiments of Henry James, and also of Joyce and Virginia Woolf—writers you will be coming to shortly.

On a strictly theoretical level, it is not difficult to show that this theory is untenable. Arnold Kettle referred to Wayne C. Booth's *The Rhetoric of Fiction* at the beginning of this unit. Booth convincingly shows that no reader in his right mind is likely to mistake what he is reading for the real world, however much the authorial manipulation is disguised. The mere presence of a beginning and an end, and the selectivity of the experience rendered, make the artificiality of fiction inevitable. Even in texts in which the author's voice seems to have been eliminated, authorial involvement is indicated in more or less secret ways—some characters are more sympathetic than others, metaphoric patterns import moral order, and so on. Explicit authorial commentary is simply more honest about the limitations of realism; and it does not follow anyway that we are limited to the views expressed in that commentary. We do not have to see Fielding as God—we may see him as a conversationalist, whose prejudices are revealed as he tells his story.

We can take this argument a stage further by saying that mimetic validity is only one dimension of the realism we value in the novel. The other dimension is its *representativeness*: the internal consistency of the narrative has to be significant in terms of the life we know. Authorial discourse builds a bridge between the particular story or character of the fiction and life in general. The elimination of authorial discourse in the interests of formal objectivity seems to commit the novel to a one-sided view of knowledge, according to which experience can be rendered only as isolated bundles of impressions whose significance is uncertain.

Nonetheless, although the passage from *Middlemarch* is a direct authorial comment, it appears to be foreshadowing precisely this kind of uncertainty about general significance. The image of unravelling certain human lots, introducing as it does a chapter analysing the complexities of Lydgate's character, suggests specifically that the 'belated historian' is limited to the particular by his awareness of those determining factors of human life which are outside the command of the individual consciousness. Thus George Eliot is anticipating Zola, whose awareness of generality was so bound up with the extra-personal determinations of character that in his works documentation becomes a more important basis of narrative than experience. On the other hand, by narrowing her own light to the immediate task, Eliot looks forward to the extreme specialization of vision seen in *What Maisie Knew*, *A Portrait of the Artist as a Young Man*, and *Mrs Dalloway*. As Lukács argued, Zola's 'naturalism' and the kind of subjectivism seen in James and his followers are not the extreme opposites they seem to be. Both result from a loss of confidence in the possibility of relating experience and the objective world in which it is placed. There is, for Lukács, a more radical difference between Balzac and Zola than there is between Zola and Joyce.

If we look more closely at Eliot's remarks, however, I think that we can do more than discern this negative connection between naturalism and subjectivism, the authorial loss of confidence; there is also a positive point of view (in turn, a development of Balzac's authorial discourse). Eliot's reflection on her own narrative task reaches for a metaphor which many critics have seen as central to the whole novel—'this particular web'. It was also in her time a very topical metaphor, whose most famous use was Darwin's. 'Plants and animals,' Darwin writes, 'most remote in the scale of nature, are bound together by a web of complex relations.' Darwin's whole theory depends on showing that the rigid categories of earlier natural historians have no stability; and his 'scale' and Eliot's 'range' are perhaps equivalent. A second important use of the metaphor, explicitly borrowed from science, was made five years before the publication of *Middlemarch*, in Walter Pater's essay 'Winckelmann', reprinted in *The Renaissance*. Necessity, Pater said, was no longer an external fate, but a 'magic web woven through and through us'. The web indicates processes which cannot be described in terms of traditional divisions between phenomena or between subject and object. Now Lydgate's development depends precisely on his emancipation from the liberal education of the gentleman into new scientific knowledge: 'the world was made new to him by a presentiment of endless processes filling the spaces blanked out of his sight by that wordy ignorance which he had supposed to be knowledge.' Eliot's difference from Fielding is paralleled by the two stages of Lydgate's education. Fielding's chat, like Lydgate's wordy ignorance, leaves out those 'endless processes'. Character, for Eliot, is 'a process and an unfolding'. Her modesty before Fielding is surely ironic. Like Lydgate, she has to become more scientific—though of course there is a further irony, in that, unlike him, she has to investigate the endless processes of his character. But the main point is that she cannot range as Fielding does, not because of a loss of confidence, but because of a concern with the interconnectedness of apparently different things. It is no longer enough for the narrator to be an observant man of common sense.

This commitment to the interpretation of experience in the light of complex processes uncovered by natural history is one shared by Balzac, Zola and Hardy. When, in *Cousin Bette*, Balzac explains the apparent eccentricity of his protagonist in terms of her peasant nature, he is shifting our attention from the notion of type to the notion of process. In *Germinal*, Zola is concerned throughout to uncover the underlying dynamic of class conflict surfacing only inarticulately in the rhetoric of political debate, the strike or the workers' subversive sexuality. Hardy comments again and again on the unconscious biological forces cutting across Tess's consciousness and capacity for decision. These are explicitly novels of processes and forces at work beneath observable social and individual characteristics.

In his book *The Order of Things*, Michel Foucault analyses the changing nature of discourse—the way succeeding epochs talk about the universe they confront—and finds, by looking at the kinds of question asked in various disciplines (natural history and political economy, for example), that whereas in the Renaissance and the Enlightenment the effort is primarily to fit phenomena into a table of categories, the predominant effort in nineteenth-century discourse is to uncover invisible laws and processes underlying the fixed, visible world. Thus knowledge is not a rational consensus formed by observation; rather, it is a reporting back from specialized, scientific experiment. Unravelling the obscure, Balzac, Zola, Eliot and Hardy register a new kind of knowledge comparable to that gained by Lydgate when he forsakes conventional books for an article on Anatomy in a Cyclopaedia. The dispassionate man of sense, whose voice greets us in the novel from *Don Quixote* to *Tom Jones*, gives way to the experimental scientist.

This 'scientificity' is specific to these writers, and, of course, their adherence to particular ideas is liable to be left behind by historical development. But the general attitude is, I think, one that is shared by other writers. If we turn for a moment to the first-person narratives of *Wuthering Heights*, *Great Expectations* and *Huckleberry Finn*, we find that this device is used to register hidden personal relationships which question the social and moral categories of the stable, visible world inherited by the protagonist. Cathy and Heathcliff, Pip and Magwitch, Huck and Jim—these are all relationships based on undeniable but unacceptable affinities. Again, the experiments in centres of consciousness which we find in James, Joyce and Woolf are a development of the first-person narrator though distanced into the third person in order to make the vision more relative, less heavy with the retrospective wisdom and personal authority that is provided by the 'I' narrating the past. But the child, the artist and the married woman are not randomly chosen: their experience is marginal to the social world in which they find themselves. It is this very marginality, however, that gives them their aesthetic authority. The withdrawal of authorial discourse does not, in fact, have the effect of making us tied merely to the empirical experience. It offers, rather, an obscure angle on the life around the protagonist. The effort of such novels is not to render the world we see but to render what we don't see.

Hardy is an exceptional and instructive case here. It is well known that he uses authorial discourse to place his protagonists' vision within a larger cosmic vision which seems to trap them in ironic illusion. There is a much-discussed instance of this in Chapter XVI of *Tess*, when the heroine is about to cross into the Valley of the Great Dairies. First, Hardy gives us Tess's view of the vale:

> When Tess had accomplished this feat she found herself to be standing on a carpeted level, which stretched to the east and west as far as the eye could reach. (Penguin ed., page 159)

It is a moment of promise. Her *effort* ('feat') is rewarded with a vision of an apparently unlimited space which is at the same time accommodating (carpets are associated with rooms that give shelter). Immediately Hardy switches to an omniscient vision which undercuts this promise:

> Not quite sure of her direction Tess stood still upon the hemmed expanse of verdant flatness, like a fly on a billiard-table of indefinite length, and of no more consequence to the surroundings than that fly. (loc. cit.)

Promise becomes uncertainty ('not quite sure'), the open space is 'hemmed', the carpeted level becomes the neutral 'flatness', and, above all, Tess becomes an inconsequential, minute fly in an indifferent space. It seems as though Hardy is working, like Fielding but pessimistically, with an ironic universality. But he calculates his effects very carefully, and this transition is abrupt enough that the reader cannot make the leap without pausing to question. If Tess is inconsequential, why are we asked to involve ourselves with her story? We already know that she herself shares this cosmic pessimism. On the other hand, she possesses 'an invincible instinct towards self-delight' which has far more reality than either her despair or her guilty conscience. For a number of reasons, then, the cosmic voice has only a relative authority. Tess's subjectivity has its validity too. What is missing here is any transition between the personal and the inhuman—a transition made in earlier Hardy novels by the voice of communal wisdom, absent in this passage and only ever present in the novel as a whole as a desultory fatalism. The whole novel depends on this tension between the subjective and the authorial voice, each showing the other's *relative* validity. I am not sentimentalizing the novel—the reader cannot help being held by Hardy's humanity, and the authorial voice acknowledges this after Tess's seduction when Hardy comments: 'But though to visit the sins of the fathers upon the children may be a morality good enough for divinities, it is scorned by average human nature; and it therefore does not mend the matter.' (See page 119.) Hereditary guilt is Darwinian as well as Judaic, but we are closer to the bewildered consciousness of Tess. What is sport for the Gods, for us is only a sign of how despicable the Gods are. As I say, Hardy is exceptional in his use of authorial discourse, but his case helps to show how the scientific author and the formal experimenter both use narrative to challenge the reality we presuppose.

I have been trying to redefine the parameters of a critical debate in order to reveal how formal issues are also historical issues. The novelist's freedom to choose his or her method is determined (not eliminated) by the need to question the given sense of the real. 'Science' may be wrong, James's formal objectivity may be impossible; but these points of view were derived from a historical impetus and enabled nineteenth-century novelists to write in the various ways they did. We should be grateful that Zola did not write like Balzac or Woolf like Eliot. Authorial discourse, its nature or its absence, is a focus for the novelist's attack on 'reality', that is, the reality we see.

Appendix

A note on realism and naturalism (by Raymond Williams)

The terms *realism* and *naturalism*, and their associated adjectives *realist* and *naturalist*, or *realistic* and *naturalistic*, are now very widely used in the discussion of literature. They are often, also, very loosely used. Given the inherent difficulty of the terms themselves, and the complexity of the questions to which they are addressed, it is not possible to provide strict universal definitions, which can be simply learned and applied. Yet there is still more looseness and confusion than there need be. It is then useful, first, to study the development of the terms in actual usage; secondly, to indicate the relations of this development to wider social changes and ideas; thirdly, to suggest how the terms themselves, including the distinctions between them, might now best be used in the discussion of literature and specifically, in this course, of novels.

Historical development of the terms

Both *realist* and *naturalist* appeared earlier, in English, than the nouns *realism* and *naturalism* from which they appear to be derived. Indeed, it is the weaker adjectival pair, *realistic* and *naturalistic*, which were derived from the nouns, especially in their later senses.

The earliest meanings of both *realist* and *naturalist* are primarily philosophical. As terms of description or criticism in art and literature they do not become common, and were perhaps not used at all, before the second half of the nineteenth century. There is then an initial problem. Are the earlier, philosophical uses irrelevant, or largely irrelevant, to the later uses in relation to art? They are certainly at some distance from them, though unevenly. It is then possible to argue that the uses in relation to art, which can be seen as referring primarily to method or technique, should be considered quite separately from the earlier philosophical uses. But this is to assume, in advance, that there are no significant connections between the philosophical positions and the literary methods. In fact we cannot assume this, either in principle or in practice. The connections, when examined, can be seen to be variable, though in some cases they are very close. But what is at issue, in this first stage of the inquiry, is itself a fundamental question, as to whether method or technique in a form of art should be studied primarily or exclusively in its own terms (a position usually defined as *formalism*) or whether one part of the study of method or technique is necessarily the study of underlying positions from which the method or technique is developed or preferred. This question is still being widely argued, but in the cases of *realism* and *naturalism*, without doubt, we have to recognize that many writers who adopted these methods did so, and said so, because they had adopted underlying general positions to which the methods were appropriate or necessary. And if this is the case, the relations between the wider and the more specialized senses of the terms have surely to be examined.

The development of *naturalist* and *naturalism* is the more straightforward of the two. It depended from the beginning on a particular sense of *nature*, and thence of the study of nature, which was consciously separating itself (though in variable ways) from the older, primarily religious senses of a divine creation. Thus we hear from early in the seventeenth century of 'atheisticall naturalists' and of those who rely only on 'morality, naturalisms and human reason'. *Naturalist* then commonly came to mean *natural philosopher*, or, as we should now say, *scientist*. Its implied opposite, at this level, was *supernaturalist*: the placing of truth beyond physical nature and human reason. The connection with *naturalism* as a nineteenth-century movement in the novel, drama and painting is then relatively direct. At the centre of this movement was the idea of applying scientific method and scientific discovery to literature and painting: whether in the particular forms of new concepts of heredity or environment, or of light or colour, or in the more general position that human experience and the physical world should be studied and interpreted in their own terms, strictly *natural* terms, thus excluding the hypothesis of some controlling or directing force beyond them, which in earlier work and methods might, if in varying ways, have to be taken account of, in composition and form. *Naturalism* then, developing relatively directly from its own earlier senses, was a simultaneous definition of both method and subject.

The development of *realist* and *realism* is very much more complicated. Instead of the simple contrast between *natural* and *supernatural*, we find at the root of these terms a double contrast: of *real* as contrasted with *imaginary*, and of *real* as contrasted with the merely *apparent*. These uses refer to questions so fundamental and so difficult that it is not surprising that, alike in philosophy and in art, the description *realist* is much more variable, and at times more slippery, than the relatively simple *naturalist* could ever be. *Realism*, a new English word in the nineteenth century, had four meanings. First, it referred to an earlier philosophical movement which had insisted on the existence of absolute universal forms—the ultimately *real*—which not only underlay but preceded and constituted observable objects. It had, however, a newer second sense which was virtually the opposite of this, taking the physical world as wholly independent of mind or spirit. Here the first use depends on the contrast of *real* with *apparent*, the second on the different contrast between *real* and *imaginary*. A third, very common use offered *realism* and *being realistic* as ways of facing 'things as they are' and not as we imagine or would prefer them to be. This sense contributed to some uses of *realism* and *realist* in literature and art. It is then quite close to the practical emphases of *naturalism*, which is of course also very close to the second sense, depending on the contrast between the *real* and the *imaginary*. However, though the terms were often close, in such ways, in their earliest period of use, the development of *realism* and *realist*, as terms of literature and art, came to include the other type of contrast, with the merely *apparent*. This was the basis for an eventual attempt to distinguish between *realism* (rejecting the imaginary but also going beyond the apparent) and *naturalism*, which, it was claimed, while rejecting the imaginary, was tied to the apparent. We shall see what substance there may be in this distinction.

The wider context of realism and naturalism

There is one certain difference between realism and naturalism. Naturalism, in its reference to art and literature, was a term deliberately chosen by a group of writers and artists, to describe and justify their position and methods. (See the quotations from Zola in Units 21–22.) Realism, on the other hand, was and has remained a much more variable and less specific description, as often applied by others as by writers and artists themselves. Thus we can fairly say that there are no naturalist novels before the Naturalist movement, but there are certainly novels that many call realist before either 'realism' or 'realist', in their applications to art and literature, had been heard of. The reason for this is that the positions and methods now grouped as 'realism' are elements of a very wide and prolonged social and intellectual history. Naturalism, by contrast, is a specific formation within this broader history. It is, then, at once more deliberate and more restricted.

In the broadest terms, realism in its modern sense is a necessary element of the bourgeois transformation of society which, while in different countries it can be traced back for many centuries, achieved its decisive new institutions and forms in the eighteenth and nineteenth centuries. One of these decisive new forms was the novel itself, in its modern sense. The prose narratives which preceded it had many elements in common with the novel's initial and subsequent practice, but we can distinguish five elements which mark the decisive transition. These are as follows:

(a) A new emphasis on *contemporary* material, as the most interesting and appropriate subject-matter

(b) A new emphasis on *indigenous* material; the preferred location of the narrative is the place to which writer and probable reader belong

(c) A broadening of *social range and inclusiveness*, so that stories are not only (or at all) about heroes and princes, but preferably about people 'like ourselves'

(d) A new *secularism*, in matters of action and interpretation, so that human actions are seen primarily or exclusively in human terms, without explicit divine or magical intervention or influence

(e) A new emphasis on *everyday language*, both for narration and for the representation of speech (which tends to become not 'dialogue' but 'conversation' or 'talk').

These five elements are now so familiar that we may, at first sight, fail to see them as distinctive. But that is because, at the most fundamental levels, the movement to which they belong has been so generally successful. If we compare the typical novel with the typical romance which preceded it, we find that the romance is different on each of these vital points: it is characteristically about the past, about the exotic, about a more limited and more socially elevated group, about some supernatural element in human affairs, and at a corresponding level of elevated style. ('Once upon a time . . . in a far country . . . a prince . . . a magic sword . . .' etc.)

What we then find, however, is that just because this general change has occurred so widely, giving most readers a basic set of expectations about what a novel should be, the description 'realist', which might reasonably be used about the movement as a whole, is in fact normally employed to describe those novels in which these elements are *most prominent*. For it is of course not the case that all novels contain all these elements, though it is rare to find a novel, which, like a romance, contains none of them. *Realist*, and more especially conscious *realism*, are then descriptions of those kinds of writing which embody these elements most thoroughly. (To avoid confusion on a minor point, it should be noted that the historical novel, since Scott, which is of course not contemporary in its choice of material, is distinct from earlier kinds of writing set in the past because of the presence of the other elements of realism; it is in this sense a realism of the past, of *history*, rather than of the quite different past of the romances.)

Realism involved many changes of method and technique, for the writer and in turn for the reader. One of the elements defined, (e), is primarily a change in writing style. But neither in its broader nor in its narrower sense is realism a primarily *technical* decision. New methods and styles followed from the new definitions of interest. It was because writers and readers were increasingly concerned with the lives of a wide range of people in their own time and place that elements (a), (b) and (c) became so important. It was because new ways of looking at the world, increasingly dependent on observation and reason, were widely replacing older supernatural kinds of interpretation and explanation that (d) became so important. The stylistic element, (e), seemed to follow from the others, but in practice it has had a wide range, from deliberate *limitation* to everyday language at its most ordinary (this has come to be called 'naturalistic') to many varied writing styles exploring the *possibilities* of every-day language. However, over this whole range, the basis of choice of a style is different from that in romance, in which a style was prescribed. Those writers who have gone furthest beyond the 'naturalistic' or the narrow sense of 'realist' have usually done so to realize more of the possibilities of 'everyday language'. (The case of Joyce is most relevant.)

The terms and the novels

All the novels discussed in this course can be seen to belong to the major realist movement in literature, in its widest sense. You may wish to consider, briefly, each of the novels in turn, and ask how closely the five elements defined are represented in them.

We can then move to the narrow and more discriminating sense of 'realist': those novels which embody these defining elements most thoroughly. This is a matter of difficult individual judgements. At times element (c), social range and inclusiveness, may seem most relevant in this distinction; for example, in the case of Jane Austen by comparison with George Eliot. Element (d), the secular, will raise difficult questions in the case of *Wuthering Heights*. The variety and range of element (e) become clear in a comparison between *What Maisie Knew* and *Huckleberry Finn*, though each is based, with very different results, on everyday language.

It may be suggested that Balzac, George Eliot and Tolstoy most clearly represent the developed forms of *realism* in its broadest sense. There are then interesting comparisons, as suggested in detail in the relevant units, with Dickens, Hardy and Henry James. An important consideration here, which is also very important in contemporary discussions of the realist novel, is the position and tone of the narrator: whether 'he' is in effect impersonal, 'above' and including his characters, or whether 'he' is an explicitly personal, inter-preting presence. What is sometimes now attacked as 'classical realism' is the supposedly omniscient, impersonal narrator. This is said to be a concealment of the author's actual position within society. How far does this seem to be true in the cases of, say, Balzac and George Eliot?

Finally, we can return to the distinction between 'realism' and 'naturalism'. In actual usage the terms have been widely confused, but the most interesting modern distinction (in Lukács and others) is, as noted above, dependent on the contrast of *real* with *apparent*, rather than of *real* with *imaginary*. Two points may then be made.

First, there is in any case a problem about *imaginary*. All 'fiction', as it has come to be called, is imagined; it does not derive its authority, as in the case of history, from independent verification, beyond its text. At the same time the 'realist' novel offers itself as, in general rather than in local detail, in broad type and tendency rather than in local and nominal correspondence and reproduction, true *to* life, true *of* life. The basis of this claim is the control of its essential composition by the five elements defined above.

Naturalism, in its broadest sense, is founded on this broad realist intention. Indeed it can best be distinguished, historically, by its exceptional emphasis on element (d), the secular, and then by a particular version of what such a secular viewpoint should be. Thus it is not true to say that naturalism was concerned only with the apparent. On the contrary, it was specifically con-cerned with what *caused* the apparent, and especially with what it took to be the laws of heredity and environment. We can say that it interpreted these laws too narrowly, or that it substituted dogmas for authentic laws. We can say that interpretation of the apparent by other and different laws, finding other and more substantial causes, is more profound and more enlightening. But we can never reasonably accuse *naturalism* (as distinct from the merely technical later sense of the *naturalistic*—the reproduction of surface detail for its own sake) of indifference to underlying causes and laws. On the contrary, we must often say that it applied such assumptions too rigidly, producing people and events as mere specimens and examples of such laws, and allowing too little room for complexity, contradiction and above all effort and initiative within the determining pressures.

That may be a valid critique of the historical movement of classical naturalism (as in Zola). But there is then a final and crucial distinction between a *realist* critique of naturalism—that its laws do not include enough reality, that it excludes real and discoverable forces—and the much weaker but very popular critique, that any attempt to find and show causes for human situations, characters and events is shallow and 'uncreative', because 'human nature' always escapes them. Indeed, it is a central position of *realism*, in its mature forms, that it is not an abstract and permanent 'human nature', but a set of real *and observable*, therefore 'narratable', processes, that create and recreate human life. It was indeed to show people as radically shaped and influenced by their natural and social environment, and by their physical heredity, but at the same time both making and remaking or trying to remake themselves within these real pressures, that the great enterprise of realist writing, and with it so many of the great novels of the world, was in both theory and practice undertaken.

References

Allott, Miriam (ed.), *Novelists on the Novel*, Routledge and Kegan Paul, 1959.

Bauer, C. and Ritt, Leonard G. (eds.), *Free and Ennobled: Source Readings in the Development of Victorian Feminism*, Pergamon, 1979.

Eliot, George, *The George Eliot Letters*, ed. Gordon S. Haight, vols. I-IX, Yale University Press, 1954–78.

Foucault, Michel, *The Order of Things: an Archaeology of the Human Sciences*, 1966; Tavistock, 1970.

Haight, Gordon S., *George Eliot: a Biography*, Oxford University Press, 1968.

Hardy, Barbara, *The Novels of George Eliot: a Study in Form*, Athlone Press, 1959; new ed., 1963.

Hobsbawm, Eric, *The Age of Capital, 1848–1875*, Weidenfeld and Nicolson, 1975.

Kettle, Arnold (ed.), *The Nineteenth-century Novel: Critical Essays and Documents* (Course Reader), 2nd ed., Heinemann Educational Books/The Open University Press, 1981.

Lubbock, Percy, *The Craft of Fiction*, Cape, 1921.

Phillpotts, Bertha S., *Edda and Saga*, Home University Library (Butterworth), 1931.

Stang, Richard, *The Theory of the Novel in England, 1850–1870*, Routledge and Kegan Paul, 1954.

Woolf, Virginia, *A Room of One's Own*, 1929; Triad/Panther (Granada), ed., 1977.

A312 The Nineteenth-century Novel and its Legacy